M000014221

BLEEDING HEART CONSERVATIVES

WHY IT'S GOOD TO BE RIGHT

ALLISON LEE PILLINGER CHOI

A POST HILL PRESS BOOK
ISBN: 978-1-68261-019-0
ISBN (eBook): 978-1-68261-020-6

BLEEDING HEART CONSERVATIVES
Why It's Good to Be Right
© 2016 by Allison Lee Pillinger Choi
All Rights Reserved

Cover Design by Quincy Alivio
Jacket Photograph by Brian Dorsey Studios

No part of this book may be reproduced, stored in a retrieval system, or transmitted by any means without the written permission of the author and publisher.

Post Hill
PRESS

Post Hill Press
275 Madison Avenue, 14th Floor
New York, NY 10016
posthillpress.com

To my dad, mom, and husband

We can't help everyone, but everyone can help someone.

—*Ronald Reagan*

TABLE OF CONTENTS

INTRODUCTION

Perhaps one of the most memorable moments of the 2012 presidential campaign was the leaked "47 percent" video where Republican candidate Mitt Romney commented on entitlements. For those of you who need a refresher, in September 2012, a liberal website released an unauthorized video clip of Romney at a fundraising dinner speaking about his campaigning efforts:

> There are 47 percent of the people who will vote for the president [Barack Obama] no matter what. All right, there are 47 percent who are with him, who are dependent upon government, who believe that they are victims, who believe the government has a responsibility to care for them, who believe that they are entitled to health care, to food, to housing, to you-name-it. That's an entitlement. And the government should give it to them. And they will vote for this president no matter what... These are people who pay no income tax... So our message of low taxes doesn't connect... And so my job is not to worry about those people. I'll never convince them they should take personal responsibility and care for their lives.[1]

---

[1]   http://www.politifact.com/truth-o-meter/statements/2012/sep/18/mitt-romney/romney-says-47-percent-americans-pay-no-income-tax/

The liberal-biased media, requiring only the most meager of kindling for content, now had gasoline to ignite a firestorm of public outrage. So widespread was this coverage that even at casual social gatherings I attended, the topic du jour was voicing one's indignation at the "callous" Republican Party.

It also highlighted to me how a specific caricature of the Republican Party was so well-engrained in the public zeitgeist. The wealth-hoarding, heartless, old, rich, conservative white man of *The Simpsons*' Mr. Burns archetype constituted the '1' on the binary Republican Party scale. The '0' was represented by the evolution-denying, gun-toting, local country bumpkin/bigot of the show's Cletus, slack-jawed-yokel archetype. There aren't many characters on *The Simpsons* that I'd like to be associated with, but those two might be the worst. Needless to say, I found myself reluctant at times to openly identify as a Republican.

That all changed one evening after a discussion with my then-boyfriend/now-husband, who I knew to be unquestionably ignorant in the field of politics. Armed with the contents of *The New York Times* article he just finished and an inflated sense of his own opinion, he proceeded to extemporize on the "47 percent" controversy by denouncing the Republican vices of greed and self-interest.

Well, I had had enough. I decided to lay out my opinion on where entitlements fit within the Republican framework (one which I am positive Governor Romney would agree). The very term entitlement suggests that it is a free privilege. I view it more as recompense for prior services rendered (e.g., the veterans of our armed forces, the elderly who have been productive members of society in their younger years, etc.) or as a safety net for those among us sincerely in need (the disabled, the working poor, those searching for employment, etc.). By ever-expanding the definition and reach of entitlements, we not only create a disincentive for those who could potentially be contributing members of society (thereby ultimately doing them a disservice), but we also dilute the effectiveness of those finite dollars by spreading them across a wider base.

The takeaway my boyfriend got from this was that it is not entitlements in principle to which I am opposed, but rather the administration and oversight of the process. The conversation ended with him asking, "So you're telling me that your Republican views on entitlements come from a sense of fairness and generosity?" To which I responded, "Liberals don't have a patent on asset redistribution. The ultimate objective of safety net entitlements should be to give more to those who need more. Just call me a bleeding heart conservative."

Who Should Read This Book?

Misguided significant others would be a large enough market for a book but reaching that target audience is not why I started putting pen to paper; the journey here was much more personal. I've identified as a conservative for a long time but it was a constructive thought exercise to step back and lay out why that is, on a topic-by-topic basis. Due to the pervasive media coverage, my thoughts on the subject of entitlements were already well formed by the time my boyfriend broached the issue. However, had he brought up security or environmental issues, my response would not have been as well structured or confident. After all, believing in a position and articulating one are two separate matters. I wanted to examine the former to be better prepared for the latter.

As I advanced in this project and started discussing it with others, I was pleasantly surprised by the breadth of interest it received. I admit the sample size was small (and probably biased towards polite agreement as the polling subjects were friends and family), but my takeaway was that the potential reader base might be larger than just its author. I've grouped who this book could be relevant to in the following categories:

The Inquisitive Millennial / Politically Uninitiated

I was born in the swing-state of Florida and raised in a family where politics was a welcome topic at the dinner table. These discussions taught me that complicated topics rarely generate an obvious right answer and therefore invite thoughtful debate. After speaking with my college-aged cousins at a family reunion, I started to question whether millennials put in the requisite deliberation before aligning themselves with a political party. It wasn't that long ago that I was a college-aged student so this spurred me to reconsider what my experience was like.

Other than brutal winters, I didn't really know what to expect as an incoming freshman. Hollywood had conditioned me into believing that only the wealthy and well-connected attended Harvard (interestingly, Hollywood misrepresentation is not uncommon, as explained later in the book), so I felt I was trespassing by virtue of a favorable clerical error at the admissions office. Thankfully I quickly found out that my classmates came from a diverse spectrum of backgrounds and were for the most part surprisingly...well, normal! The majority of the first few weeks were spent making new and diverse friends but freshmen are also introduced to the wide array of extracurricular activities during this period. The Institute of

Politics (IOP) was one of the clubs that had a vocal presence on campus and I intended on joining.

I was hoping that the discussions at the IOP would in some small way connect my new life at Harvard with my family dinner table. Unfortunately, that wasn't to be. The small sample set of IOPers I met with were outspoken, dogmatic, and overwhelmingly liberal. I felt that ideas which fell "right of center" were not meant to be discussed but rather attacked. Statistics, quotes, and historical precedence were wielded like weapons and gave the environment a *Thunderdome* feel. There was a small but brave contingent of Republicans putting up a fight but at the time I was not interested in joining that outnumbered battle. I bid a hasty retreat and was back to my normal mix of classes, friends, tennis, and all the other activities that I have such fond memories of today. I don't regret walking away from the IOP but I do feel a bit cheated that as a moderate Republican, the college campus was not exactly an encouraging environment for one to express or develop right-leaning political thought. In fact, one of my biggest takeaways from college was that the moderate Republican is either an endangered species or a highly camouflaged one.

But in retrospect, I actually think that was a good thing. College was a formative period for the development of my political opinions but it did not happen due to staged interactions at the IOP. It came from late night conversations with classmates who were first-generation immigrants. It came from comforting friends going through difficult personal times. It came from earning a minimum wage with part-time jobs. And it came subtly through the myriad of experiences that come from transitioning from a child to an adult. But this development was only possible because I kept an open mind throughout; and that is where I take issue with "kids these days."

When did it become "a given" that you're either liberal or ignorant on college campuses? My theory is that this notion was solidified when comedy shows became the preferred source of news for the younger audience. Jon Stewart, Stephen Colbert, and John Oliver, comedians who report on topics with satirical mockery, are now viewed as the political news authority (with Stewart recently topping network news anchors as "the most trusted newscaster in America").[2] Taking a short video clip (sometimes out of context), mimicking the subject of said clip in an obnoxious tone, then commenting with smug piousness, is not news — it's entertainment. As I said earlier, politics often revolve around complicated topics that have no easy answers. To assume one can arrive at a conclusion in a neat five-minute segment is not only arrogant, it's dangerous.

Which brings us back to my family reunion, where I'm listening to two cousins tell me everything there is to know about the tragedies of income inequality... in three minutes. Naturally, my knee-jerk reaction was to say, "Listen, punks, you have no idea what you're talking about." But I took a deep breath and before I said anything, a quote hit me. In the immortal words of Whitney Houston, "I believe the children are our future." And if you believe this, it seems today as if there won't even be a conservative party in that future by maintaining the status quo.

I decided to take a different approach with my cousins. I started by agreeing with them. "You're right," I said, "structural income inequality is categorically immoral in my opinion." My section

---

2   http://time.com/3704321/jon-stewart-daily-show-fake-news/

on Income Inequality outlines how the rest of our conversation went but the conclusion was comforting. Were they entirely convinced of my position by the end of our discussion? No. But did they realize and fully admit that there were many complicated questions they did not ask themselves? Yes. And it was clear they wanted to learn more because they understood that conveniently blaming "greedy" Republicans was not only simplistic but wrong.

It's a one-sided fight in terms of winning the minds of millennials, and liberals have found an efficient, effective, and even profitable method of doing so with satirical news. I make no claims that this book is by any means the answer (actually, presenting a physical book to a millennial may seem dreadfully old-fashioned). However, the subjects we are about to discuss deserve more than 140 characters and can't be resolved by getting 1,000 Facebook likes. It's a long shot but my hope is that younger audiences can be reached by explaining conservative opinions on major fiscal, social, and foreign policy issues from a modest and compassionate perspective. The book is divided into easily digestible sections that can be picked up and put down, topic by topic in the order which most interests the reader. Hopefully it can be used as a reference manual to those millennials who, after viewing a *Daily Show* segment, have the inquisitiveness and courage to ask, "Well, what's the other side?"

The Camouflaged Conservative

We're not talking about Navy Seals here. I'm referring to those individuals who identify themselves as either "socially liberal/ fiscally conservative," right-leaning centrists, Rockefeller Republicans, or Libertarians. Trust me, I get it. I moved to New

York City after college and even our mayor at the time no longer wanted to call himself a conservative.

The Left has done an excellent job of simplifying political party allegiance into two hot button topics: gay marriage and abortion. Where you stand on the economy, national security, education, etc., is all an afterthought. It's an easy litmus test. If you are against marriage equality and a woman's right to choose, you are a Republican... and a bigot, homophobe, and misogynist.

Well, stereotypes can sometimes be unfair. I joined the labor force not too long before the start of the 2008 presidential campaigns and my employer was Goldman Sachs. Contrary to popular opinion about Wall Street investment banks, my firm's PAC donated more to the Obama campaign than any other company PAC with the exception of the University of California.[3] In a firm so focused on risk versus reward, it was not lost upon me that espousing my conservative beliefs would be a bad bet. After a few years I found my way further along the liberal spectrum when I worked in the corporate office of the fitness company Equinox. Perhaps it was because I was no longer a doe-eyed, fresh-out-of-college newbie, but I felt so much more comfortable in my own skin there despite the liberal milieu. After all, good people are good people no matter what race, creed, or even political affiliation.

I made many close friends during my time at Equinox and conversations outside the conference room would eventually stumble upon some current event topic that had political

---

[3]   http://www.cnn.com/2010/POLITICS/04/20/obama.goldman.donations/

relevance. Many of my friends there were liberal but even those who fell right of center would insist they were not conservative. When I would ask what the aversion was to identifying as conservative, the answer would invariably start with, "Well, I'm gay" or "I'm a feminist" and we'd get into a discussion about gay marriage or abortion.

Marriage equality and a woman's right to choose are emotional topics for both sides. Your viewpoint on these subjects may not necessarily stem from a place of logic but rather from a personal or religious stance. I've found that debates are only constructive when both parties agree upon a common set of values and argue under the same parameters. When you disagree on something elemental, there is no debate to be had. I've found that once you move past those third rails of gay marriage and abortion, these camouflaged conservatives agree with many Republican positions. In full disclosure, I actually support marriage equality and oppose a staunchly strict pro-life policy. This doesn't preclude me from being conservative. In fact, when asked how I can identify with the party which traditionally disconnects with me here, I explain that I much prefer to motivate my party to progress on specific issues than to see my country regress under the alternative party.

This book is written on behalf of the tribes that include moderate conservatives, right-leaning centrists, "socially liberal/fiscally conservative," Rockefeller Republicans, libertarians, et al., in hopes of uniting us under the banner Bleeding Heart Conservatives. BHCs are conservatives who base political opinions on analytical and moral thought to determine the best practices that will benefit the individual and, in turn, overall society. Our thought process is grounded in conservative-minded principles (not necessarily Republican Party ideology), and is sensitive to but not altogether influenced by emotion. We may not align with *every* endorsed Party platform; however, we identify with broader conservative principles and apply them accordingly to arrive at our political stances and ultimately our affiliation. These viewpoints reflect a belief that thoughtful Republicans can embrace and non-Republicans can respect, thereby ending the perpetuation of negative conservative stereotypes.

Republicans in Want of a Refresher

As I mentioned earlier, the process of examining political issues topic by topic has been both an enlightening and enjoyable exercise. Republicans cannot live on Fox News alone, and stepping away from current events to focus on the philosophical underpinnings has renewed my confidence in the conservative movement.

As a board member of the Women's National Republican Club, I spend more than my fair share of time with life-long conservatives, and I've noticed two common traits. First, our members are patriots with a deep sense of civic responsibility and love of country. Second, our members largely view being Republican as a central characteristic to who they are as people.

When something is so engrained in you that it becomes second nature, there is a risk you stop examining it. I played competitive tennis from Juniors to NCAA, and I know how to hit a forehand. When my husband asks me for tips on his forehand, I respond, "You do this <demonstrate forehand> and it kinda feels right, you know?" No, he doesn't know and I haven't analyzed the mechanics of my swing in 15 years, so it's difficult for me to explain.

This problem can also apply to life-long Republicans. You may have come to your conservative views in a well-thought-out way. But after so many years of identifying as a Republican, you may not have examined those thoughts in quite some time and it may be difficult to articulate when asked. I'm reminded of a quote by the poet John Dryden: "We first make our habits, and then our habits make us." This book is an opportunity to take back control of those habits. Time passes and people change. Perhaps in thoroughly examining specific topics you may surprise yourself and find that your viewpoints have shifted as well.

Two Caveats: What This Book Is Not

It ain't Shakespeare. I have no formal training in writing and have never even considered it a casual hobby. The framework of *Bleeding Heart Conservatives* came from notes intended solely for internal consumption. The brief flurry of confidence which compelled me to reach out to publishers dissolved into self-doubt once my proposal was accepted. But each time I felt foolish or self-conscious about my writing, I decided that I'd gladly endure any lengths of literary criticism to get my message across. How could it hurt to have more open-minded and clear-thinking conservatives speak up? *BHC* hopes to serve as a voice for everyday moderate conservatives, invigorate jaded, self-conscious, and camouflaged conservatives, as well as enlighten curious apoliticals and truly open-minded liberals.

It's also not a statistical report. BHC believes that the individual human spirit lies at the core of conservative philosophy. As such, I deliberately avoid gravitating towards quantitative statistics for two reasons. One, many excellent books have already been written (by authors smarter than I) which use statistical evidence to support conservative policies. For an especially enlightening read, I direct you to *Unintended Consequences* by Edward Conard. But more importantly, hard numbers weren't the central reason I gravitated towards conservative philosophy. A belief in fairness to all, a deep appreciation for freedom, and common sense were much more instrumental. BHC relies on those qualities and a clear message over prose and numbers.

So with that, I invite you to read, deliberate, challenge, and most importantly discuss the topics to follow. Obviously, the ideal goal is for the majority of readers to align with my overall positions. However, for those who do not, the other goal is that you understand how my views come from a place of compassion and with the best interest of our society at heart. As cliché as it is, I will leave you with one final quote that I hope you adopt as I have through sharing my thoughts. Walter Annenberg, whose philanthropic work has provided financial aid for many students at Harvard, once said the following: "I shall participate, I shall contribute, and in so doing, I will be the gainer."

PART I
THE MEANS

Everyday citizens, whether conservative, liberal, independent, or otherwise, essentially have the same positive hopes for themselves, their families, our society, and the world. Qualities like freedom, safety, and self-sufficiency are just a few basic common goals. *So then, what is the key element which differentiates political groups?* First, it is certainly *not* what is in our wallets or the colors of our skin (just ask liberal hedge fund billionaire George Soros or conservative African-American Congresswoman Mia Love). Rather, the key difference is our opinion on the most effective avenues to achieve those bipartisan hopes. If Americans could come to recognize that our end goals are generally the same, with the means left up for debate, then that would help calm the tension which enables irrational emotion to sabotage otherwise productive opportunities for discussion.

With a renewed focus on addressing those means, the negative judgments and wrongly assumed end goals (e.g., conservatives block women's rights and prevent minorities from voting) will not pose irrelevant distractions from achieving the real goal — that is, not the political win but rather the best solution for the citizenry. And like many policy solutions, the best ones may come from debates and compromises involving differing political ideas; after all, this is how bleeding heart conservatives arrive at our personal politics. Our politics are formed by considerations of various means as espoused by past and present policies, lawmakers, and thought leaders from all points along the spectrum. From here we find that we favor conservative-minded means. Nevertheless, our overall stance reflects a combination of means which we believe can best achieve effective solutions for all. In the "religion" of politics, platforms are not commandments, politicians are not deities, and party observance is not judged by a cleric. Rather, our conservative stance is thoughtfully molded by variable means and is not defined (or deterred) by a single hot topic, a politicized controversy, a bombastic gaffe-prone politician, or a late night comedic jab.

While personal politics are customizable given the wide variety and complexity of issues, there is one particular overarching debate regarding the means which essentially drives political association toward conservative or liberal. The emphasis placed on the individual versus government often sums up the contrast between the two political groups' preferred means. In other words, conservatives support greater individual freedoms which require assurances of government limitations, whereas liberals support greater government involvement which inherently limits individual freedoms. These concepts are often referenced by the terms "limited government" versus "big government."

We view a government of limited control and restricted power as critical to preserving the basis for a free and prosperous society. In kind, a limited government is a critical means to enabling other principles of conservatism. Accordingly, we apply these principles to fiscal, social, and foreign policy issues to arrive at our positions. While many of our principles overlap with liberal ideals (not surprisingly, as again we typically have the same ultimate goals), the overarching principle means of *limited government* is the unique foundation of conservatism and of our country.

Conservative Principles	
Accountability	Morality (religious or secular)
American Exceptionalism	Opportunity
Belief in the Individual	Patience
Charity and Volunteerism	Patriotism
Civic Duty	Peace through Strength
(Conscious) Capitalism[1]	Personal Choice
Consequences (intended and unintended)	Personal Responsibility
Constitutional Rights	Regard for Human Life
Efficacy	Resilience
Equality (for all and favoritism to none)	Respect (inward and outward)
Fiscal Responsibility	Rule of Law
Foundation in Family and Community	Sacrifice
Free Market (competition)	Security (personal and public)
Freedom	Self-empowerment
Independence	Self-reliance
Integrity	Solidarity
Meritocracy	Well-prepared Military
Limited Government	

---

[1]   http://www.consciouscapitalism.org

Limited Government

The belief in limited government encapsulates conservative politics. A limited government, typically in reference to the *federal* government, is a humble form of governance (in contrast to that from which our Founding Fathers disaffected). The restrained power and control of politicians serving in a smaller government capacity gives way to private citizens' self-empowerment — to live, learn, and work in a less regulated, free market society. Under a limited government, state and local governments play a more integral role, which enables private citizens (constitutionally referenced as "We the people") to be involved and have their wills understood.

A limited government does not imply *no* government. Conservatives want a limited yet meaningfully sufficient government to maintain *necessary* functions for public assistance and administration. For example, government jurisdictions include enforcing law and order, protecting national security, and administering tax revenues to fund public initiatives (e.g., highways and social safety nets). A limited government strikes a delicate balance between authority and free will/free markets. We need a government to assist in the dynamics of natural free markets, for example through enforcing property rights and contract law. At the same time, we need a limited government to avoid crossing the threshold which takes rules, regulations, and restrictions into intrusive and ultimately damaging territory. As noted by Arthur C. Brooks in *The Conservative Heart*, "Government must work with human nature instead of trying to override it."[2]

---

[2]   http://arthurbrooks.com/book/the-conservative-heart/

Big government (also referenced as "nanny state") is the liberal preference over a limited government. Big government enables federal government officials to more heavily influence and orchestrate social and fiscal dynamics. The far-left version of this is known as socialism and a further degeneration of this known as communism are both philosophies staunchly averse to limited government. Liberals believe that government is more responsible and effective than the private citizen in creating a better — by way of "fairer" — society. Big government oversees the citizenry and ensures that they live, work, and earn in a manner judged righteous by government's standards. In theory, big governance practices might be presumed reasonable given that major U.S. government officials are typically majority-elected and sworn to serve and represent their constituents. However, in practice a few realities disrupt this ideal liberal model. First, many government officials are not elected but rather appointed or hired (cronyism, anyone?). Second and more significant, all too often we see politicians on both sides of the aisle mislead, change positions, lie, cheat, submit to lobbyists and bribery, etc. So why place greater confidence in and grant excessive authority to people who are really just private-citizens-turned-public-politicians? Conservatives do not. As noted by human rights activist Gary Kasparov, in response to the many liberals today pushing for socialism in the U.S., "Once you give power to the government it is nearly impossible to get it back, and it will be used in ways you cannot expect."[3] This observation comes in large part from his experience living in the USSR and Russia, under socialist-style government with a state-run distribution system. Unlike the private individual, an individual representing government

---

3   http://www.thedailybeast.com/articles/2016/03/10/garry-kasparov-
     hey-bernie-don-t-lecture-me-about-socialism-i-lived-through-it.html

can legally use force to authoritatively push forward its agenda. Our belief in the appropriate nature of a *limited* government goes well beyond a philosophical ideology valuing private individual freedoms and personal choice. From a very practical standpoint we are relatively more confident in the nature of local private citizenry than in the nature of government politicians. We view autonomous individuals as being more rational and efficient than authoritative bureaucrats.

The quintessential limited government and free market philosophy, libertarianism (specifically, contemporary U.S. libertarianism), often serves as an attractive political ideal to many conservatives. Libertarians generally support an exceptionally "laissez-faire political philosophy advocating only minimal state intervention in the lives of citizens."[4] Their vision of free market limited government is more extensive than that of conservatives. They believe government should hold virtually no place in the personal lives of private citizens. For this reason, libertarianism is typically categorized as a sub-party under the larger conservative umbrella. Conservatives might selectively enter into libertarian territory on specific issues or dive right into the movement.

With comprehensive support for free will without government intervention, some socially relevant libertarian opinions land on the left side of the political spectrum. As a result, libertarians often identify as "fiscally conservative and socially liberal." For example, same-sex marriage, abortion, and foreign military assistance are social areas where libertarians typically align more with liberal opinion. However, the same libertarian philosophy

---

4   http://www.oxforddictionaries.com/us/definition/american_english/libertarianism

applied to social issues of gun ownership and health care, for instance, elicits opinions which are not at all liberal; opinions on these matters may even veer more politically right than conservative perspective. So like much in politics, the positions of conservative, liberal, and in between libertarian proponents are not nearly so cut and dry. In fact, a 2014 Pew poll found that almost one-quarter of self-identified libertarians had no idea what the word means.[5] Probably more certain than the mainstream understanding of libertarianism is that in today's pop-political environment, identifying as a libertarian carries a sense of deeper political thinking than one who resorts to choosing between a tired and rigid two-party option... or worse, a cranky old out-of-touch conservative. Regardless of truly believing in libertarianism or simply indulging in the label, identifying as libertarian comes with the convenient perk of bypassing the tensions manifested from today's politically dichotomous culture.

Why then wouldn't the bleeding heart conservative, a believer in limited government and relatively liberal on social issues of gay marriage and early term pro-choice abortion, identify as libertarian? While we have shared beliefs around free markets and limited government, libertarianism supports a *very* free market with *very* limited government relative to that of conservatism. We find libertarian philosophy to be perceived as lacking an element of civic duty. Civic duty is something we view as desirable and necessary to American society. For instance, conservatives view foreign relations, national security, gun-related background checks, safety net programs, abortion term limits (barring extenuating circumstances), and

---

5   http://www.pewresearch.org/fact-tank/2014/08/25/in-search-of-
         libertarians/

equal opportunity assurances as within the limited realms of which law and government ought to be engaged; libertarians view government intervention in these areas to be relatively less appropriate. Within the BHC fundamental belief in limited government, these "limited" responsibilities are ones which we hold in high regard.

In spite of the nuances between conservativism and libertarianism, it may still be more palatable for some (read: socially acceptable) to label right-leaning politics as almost anything other than conservative or Republican. Besides being inaccurate, we see a drawback to being lured by less controversial labels, such as libertarian or independent, as a result of social pressure. Conservatism needs now more than anything (aside from a 2016 GOP win for the White House!) support from its everyday mainstream conservatives. In other words, we should not shy from political talk when the opportunity presents itself. Through contributing to the collective everyday voice of reasonable conservatives, hopefully referencing viewpoints laid out in this book, we can develop the critical mass to refresh and rebrand the conservative message. From here others can discover what we see as so remarkable: all that conservative principles have done for our country and all they can continue to do for our country.

PART II
FISCAL

The Economy

In the spirit of America's emphasis on promoting individual freedom and prosperity, the government's involvement in the economy was always intended to be one of limited power. In other words, a free market environment with limited government regulation will optimize Americans' abilities to live freely and conduct business successfully. We respect the necessary purposes our *limited* government serves within our economy; however, we are concerned over the increasingly frequent and severe ways government has been imposing its fiscal influence. Excessive spending, undisciplined borrowing, overbearing ineffective tax hikes, and onerous regulations are principal political concerns for conservatives. A major reason for many Americans to broadly identify as conservative centers on our perspective regarding economic issues — in short, that we believe in the overarching potentials fostered by a largely free market system and by fiscal responsibility (on the part of the government as well as the individual). And as noted accordingly in the Social part of this book (see Part III), we recognize how fiscal issue successes often carry over to positively influence major social issue successes.

Capitalism

Liberal Accusation: Capitalism works only in favor of the wealthy 1%.

BHC Counter: I truly believe that capitalism ultimately works in favor of anyone of any background who demonstrates work ethic, rational choices, sacrifice, and patience. I believe in the virtues of capitalism because I believe in the individual and his or her capabilities; specifically, that private individuals, not the government, have shown to be the most effective engineers of personal success, job creation for others, economic growth, and a prosperous society for all. In tandem with this, I believe government is necessary to ensure basic capitalistic principles and laws, such as private property and competitive markets (e.g., no price-setting monopolies), are observed by private individuals. Cooperatively, these ideas are what make American capitalism — that is, capitalism framed within the constitutional parameters of limited government regulation. The capitalist model practiced in the U.S. has over the long-term shown to be an optimal combination of free enterprise with limited but necessary governance to ensure ethical commerce.

Conservatives believe capitalism enables the spirit of the individual. Capitalism is an economic system in which a country's trade and industry are controlled by private individuals or companies rather than by the government.[1] Under capitalism, every individual regardless of background, race, gender, or ethnicity is fiscally free from government control (with reasonable exceptions, for example, of certain taxes) and free

---

[1] http://www.oxforddictionaries.com/us/definition/american_english/capitalism

to pursue economic fulfillment as he or she sees prudent (e.g., accountant, cook, architect, plumber). These individuals include those all along the socio-economic spectrum: from the upper class to those striving to enter the working class, from native to foreign-born. American capitalism has called on impoverished foreigners immigrating to the U.S. to work and realize their American dream. The capitalist fundamentals of American society have empowered the potential of the individual and in turn laid foundations for others, including generations to follow. The empowerment of capitalism does not start and end with the individual entrepreneur; rather, it catalyzes a potentially perpetual multiplier effect, involving hired workers, promoted workers, workers-turned-entrepreneurs and so on. All of these working individuals along the way contribute to the greater success of society.

Our positive interpretation of capitalism is unfortunately not shared by all. Anti-capitalists on the Left, such as the 99% Occupy Wall Street protesters, personify capitalism with greedy white male executives in a board room plotting to make themselves richer and the poor poorer (and kick puppies at the same time). The misunderstanding of capitalism as greedy, only serving to make wealthy people wealthier and poor people poorer, stems from a very misguided application of "zero-sum game" theory. This theory is either naively or deceptively applied here by many liberals. A zero-sum game requires that the success of one must come at the expense of another — competition in its most extreme form. In other words, if all the money in the economy were represented by a pie chart, then an increase of the one slice occurs simultaneously with the decrease of another slice. However, the fact is that the zero-sum game concept does not apply to American capitalism. The capitalist pie is not static in size; rather, it grows (e.g., from a 10″ to a 16″

pizza pie) such that all participants in the larger-scale economy see their pie slices increase. Under the general dynamics of capitalist free market competition, the U.S. economy grows, thriving domestically and internationally.

Competition is a basic tenet of capitalism. With competition, a product or service prevails until it is replaced by a better or less expensive version more desired by consumers. The more desirable product or service is delivered by either the same company or a competing company (e.g., Apple versus Samsung). We as consumers all benefit from this dynamic, though we probably take this for granted. Each wave of improvement makes consumers, industry, and society better off. For example, we have seen the landline phone made obsolete by the cell phone, which in sequence is being made obsolete by the smart phone. With each wave of competition-inspired innovation, goods and services, new and old, become better and less expensive.

Because of capitalism's essential element of robust competition, there is inevitably a component of failure — in the grand scheme of "real life" this is not a bad thing. We do not view failure as intrinsically unfavorable, since the "idea of capitalism is not just success but also the failure that allows success to happen."[2] Capitalism allows an individual to bounce back and continue to seek success, especially after learning from prior failed efforts. And in the case of very difficult scenarios requiring bounce-back support, the American capitalist economy is equipped with safety net tools such as bankruptcy law, unemployment benefits, and welfare — means-tested safety nets as supported by conservatives (see Welfare section). These safety nets are

---

2   http://www.brainyquote.com/quotes/quotes/p/pjorour447316.html

guaranteed to citizens who have fallen on hard times in spite of their best efforts and wish to regain their fiscal independence. Given our nation's long-term track record, as well as assurances of a society-backed safety net, Americans should be confident that their aspirations can be attained or reclaimed through hard work, rational decisions, patience, and sacrifice. Under the freedoms of American capitalism, these qualities provide the tools which enable self-empowerment.

The 2008 financial collapse was an infamous time for capitalism. Many liberals used this situation to further propagate a belief that capitalism is made by and for greedy evil rich people. While we largely disagree with the essence of this sentiment, we can in one sense agree — we do not blame capitalism for the negative consequences, but rather we blame negligent and bad people making irresponsible decisions. Not surprisingly, this is similar to our stance on gun violence — it is not the gun which is the inherent problem but rather the person pulling the trigger (see Gun Control section). In both cases, appropriately applied limited government regulation can help limit trouble; but of course, inappropriately applied government overregulation causes other troubles. The world has experienced financial collapses over a range of economic backdrops — from capitalism here to socialism in Greece. These cases do not have economic systems in common, but what they do have in common are people at the individual and government levels making naively or unethically irresponsible decisions. Conservatives believe that anyone (including the rich) who negligently or criminally acted for financial gain to the detriment of others should face consequences and penalties. With regard to consequences, many liberals may not realize or acknowledge that capitalism in its purest form would *not* have supported the government bailouts of the big banks (so much for staunch conservatism being in the pocket of big money). Rather, the government's handling of the aftermath of the financial crisis integrated positions coming from both political rationales.

The liberal alternative to capitalism is socialism, a system in which the production and distribution of goods are controlled substantially by the government rather than by private enterprise.[3] Under socialism the government wields much more power, influencing if not orchestrating economic and social matters such as income redistribution. Most goods and services are subsidized or "free," but these actually come at a cost — both fiscal as well as social costs. There are many well-run countries, such as those of Scandinavia and Canada, which operate under an economy with certain socialist characteristics (e.g., very high taxes) but are balanced with capitalist business-friendly qualities (e.g., less regulation, arguably less regulated than in the U.S.). Nevertheless, this does not wholly reflect the fundamental virtues of freedom and individuality by which the U.S. was founded. We view a socialist government as one which limits a citizen's economic freedom and individual potential. This consequently limits the ability for the greater society to optimize its potential and fully prosper.

Beyond the more fiscal impacts on the individual and greater society, socialism effectively puts government on a pedestal by granting politicians excessive authority over the people it governs — or, more fittingly, supervises. A socialist government looks to ensure all citizens earn similar incomes to prevent a subset of citizens from earning *too much* income. This government is also in charge of determining how much is "too much" and

---

[3]   http://dictionary.reference.com/browse/socialism

what quantifies "fair" (not unlike a parent-child relationship). When political corruption is as rampant as corporate scandal, it seems counterintuitive for anyone (including liberals) to be less trusting of a person working as an entrepreneur and more trusting of a person governing as a political bureaucrat. Ultimately, people are people whether they work in the private sector or the public sector, and they will act as they so choose. At least under capitalism, the individual is, by definition, much more in control of his or her own destiny rather than under the authority of an overly-centralized government system where control has the greater potential to go awry.

Many liberal supporters of socialism are quite vocal in their disgust over the wealth amassed via capitalism by business owners, entrepreneurs, corporate executives, and financiers. Recently in the form of Occupy Wall Street/1%-protesters (ironically, who protest via capitalist-backed technologies), liberals hypocritically overlook the wealth amassed by musicians, athletes, or actors when voicing discontent with the 1%-ers of free market capitalism. Popular celebrities like Beyonce, LeBron James, and Matt Damon have earned their successes through employing quintessential capitalist qualities (again, ironic given their left-wing endorsements) through realizing their talent (rational choices), working very hard (work ethic), and competing against others (competition) to be top on the charts, on the court, and on screen. And we see that they certainly enjoy many of the fruits of their labor, as well as donate a portion of those fruits — but at their discretion. The everyday non-celebrities doing the same in an office, a lab, a store, an operating room, a courtroom, or even a boardroom equally deserve to work for, appreciate, and employ their personal successes as they see proper.

Taxes

Liberal Accusation: You do not believe in paying your fair share.

BHC Counter: I believe that everyone has a right to keep their fair share of their earned income. The remaining share of a worker's earned income should provide tax revenues needed to efficiently fund public services and programs. I believe an appropriate tax schedule is required to support a functioning and civil society. Taxes well-spent enable citizens to maximize their freedom and the opportunities available to them as Americans.

Conservatives believe all Americans ought to pay taxes at a necessary and reasonable rate, with the expectation that these taxes are being efficiently used to fund constitutional and fiscally responsible initiatives (see Federal Budget & Spending section). We want money raised through taxes to fund projects and initiatives, from highways for all to welfare for those in need, which support practical public operations (*not* "bridges to nowhere"). Conservatives take serious issue when federal tax dollars are not only excessively taken from workers, but then also wasted on inefficient projects — sadly, the practice has become synonymous with political bureaucracy.

Nevertheless, liberals continue to slanderously criticize conservatives over our views on taxation, specifically for our alleged greedy opposition to paying our "fair share." The slander is so outrageous that some left-wing media personalities (e.g., Michael Moore, MSNBC's Chris Matthews) suggested the Tea Party, a subset of the Republican Party, was responsible for the 2013 Boston bombing because the attack took place on Tax Day, April 15th. These liberal personalities had much less to say on the matter once the identities and motives of the extremist Islamic terrorists' behind the plot were revealed.

The ugly politics of taxation, specifically with regard to the liberal portrayal of the conservative stance on the issue, have become distorted and, as a result, divisive. Class warfare is manifested accordingly: a socioeconomic problem exists; politicians call for taxes to fund solutions in the form of public programs; the socioeconomic problem continues despite a history of funding; politicians call for more taxes to fund these same programs; and the problem continues or worsens, at which point liberal politicians call for higher income-earning citizens to pay even more taxes (i.e., the politicized yet ambiguous ever-increasing "fair share") to fund more "fixing." When the assumption is that more taxpayer money will fix societal problems, the potentials for increased taxes (in terms of rates and prevalence) seem limitless. Consequential public perception is that higher-earning citizens are held responsible for fixing the problem. It is then only "logical" that those responsible for fixing it must be those to blame for causing or at least perpetuating it.

In 1980, the bottom 90 percent of taxpayers paid 50.72 percent of income taxes. In 2011 (the most recent year the data is available), the bottom 90 percent paid 31.74 percent of taxes. On the flip side, the top 1 percent paid 19.05 percent of taxes in 1980 and [paid] 35.06 percent of taxes [in 2011].[4]

The call for paying "fair share" is classic (and catchy) liberal rhetoric for the general belief that people who earn higher

4   http://taxfoundation.org/blog/top-1-percent-pays-more-taxes-
     bottom-90-percent

paychecks should pay more than they already pay in taxes. And with a dictionary definition of "fair" being "in accordance with the rules or standards; without cheating"[5] it only makes sense that conservatives would be ignorantly characterized by the Left as greedy tax-evading cheats (à la *The Simpsons'* Mr. Burns). We of course have a few issues with the liberal (especially the socialist) vision of "fair share," but an overarching one involves the conflict of interest for government to exploit a very subjective outcry for "fair" and who must pay that "share" to the government. Rather, we see the matter from the opposite perspective: "fair" should be applied to hard working Americans earning their keep. To "earn one's keep" requires earning your salary and, as importantly, keeping an appropriate share of your salary to do with your money as you wish (e.g., consumption, investment, charity, saving). The complementary share would go toward paying taxes, which we view as practical and necessary to support a civil and functioning society. The terms "fair" and "appropriate" can both be interpreted subjectively, but the nuances can be differentiated by encapsulating each party's *general* approach to taxation. The liberal approach looks at what an individual has and from there determines what rate of that should be taken based on what they deem as fair. On the other hand, the conservative approach focuses on what a society needs and from that end goes on to determine an appropriate tax rate based on a principle of equality. This by no means implies an equal dollar amount from every worker; rather, an equal percentage plan from every worker (known as a flat tax system), or more likely a plan close to it.

---

[5]   http://www.oxforddictionaries.com/us/definition/american_english/fair

Many conservatives support a flat tax plan — with one universal tax rate — for all private citizens and families. Through this plan, wealthy Americans would still be paying more in total dollars — a significant majority share of the federal wallet — and poor Americans would still be paying less. However, under a flat tax plan the government does not take more than *its* fair share from any hard-working Americans. Rather, hard-working Americans can keep their fair share with the freedom to independently decide how to budget, spend, save, invest and, yes even donate their earned income. The assumption that privately earned wealth does not serve the underprivileged without government-forced tax redistribution is categorically false. The reality is that most Americans do voluntarily choose to allocate a portion of their income to charitable donations.[6] With our innate culture of charity, philanthropy, and volunteerism, the U.S. remains atop the World Giving Index.[7] And to the surprise of many, statistics have found that conservatives, who on average earn 6% less than liberals, actually donate to charity 30% more.[8]

An overall simplification of the tax code, like one offered through a flat tax plan, would make the annual anticipation of the tax filing process less intimidating and more transparent. Calculating end of year federal taxes owed to the government should not be a brain teaser and certainly not a mystery. Tax credits and deductions would also be streamlined and scrubbed of questionable loopholes — "perks" typically reserved for wealthier individuals with the resources to legally avoid certain

---

6   http://www.gallup.com/poll/166250/americans-practice-charitable-giving-volunteerism.aspx

7   https://www.cafonline.org/about-us/publications/2014-publications/2014-infographic

8   http://reason.com/archives/2006/12/19/the-giving-gap

tax responsibilities. Every citizen should more or less anticipate the amount they owe and why — and independently file without feeling the need to hire professional help.

With regard to corporate taxes, conservatives believe the current U.S. tax plan is unfairly and counterintuitively burdensome on corporations. Big companies and small businesses are job creators which provide the vast majority of Americans the opportunities to make a living. In the U.S., these businesses are required to pay corporate income taxes at rates higher than in any other developed economy.[9] Consequently many U.S. businesses have relocated or incorporated in other countries with less onerous corporate tax rates (e.g., Pfizer, Burger King, Michael Kors). With these moves abroad, jobs and economic growth which should be in the U.S. are instead benefitting other countries. When corporate taxpayers leave the system, the U.S. loses a significant amount of tax revenues which could have been realized under reasonable tax rates (e.g., at least on par with that of other business-friendly countries). We want to see corporate tax rates lowered to levels which inspire businesses and entrepreneurs to establish, grow, and even relocate here.

Federal Budget and Spending

Liberal Accusation: You want government to cut funding public programs for Americans.

BHC Counter: I want our government to demonstrate fiscal responsibility by creating a viable budget and then from there responsibly spend to fund necessary public programs. The

---

9   http://www.bloomberg.com/infographics/2014-09-18/tax-runaways-tracking-inversions.html

exorbitant federal spending habits over the past few decades have resulted in mounds of debt with very disappointing social and economic results to show for it (e.g., low education scores and high poverty rates). It is well-past time for our government to take a responsible look at where and how it spends Americans' taxes and borrowed money. This would involve reducing funds for inefficient programs and altogether eliminating unnecessary programs which were bureaucratically (read: irresponsibly) created. A disciplined practice like this will incrementally move our national debt towards reasonable levels as well as make more funding available for efficient and effective programs. Fiscal responsibility is not a practice for the sake of being stingy; rather, it is a disciplined means of being solvent for everyone's benefit.

Setting a federal budget, similar to setting a personal budget, can be boiled down to three variables: 1) estimation of funding needs for public programs, emergencies, and projects which require taxpayer money (e.g., welfare, public housing, disaster relief, military, roads, parks); 2) forecast of tax revenues from U.S. taxpayers and debt borrowings from lenders to fund the costs of these public initiatives; and 3) projection of the debt repayment schedule to lenders. Unfortunately, our government has not demonstrated basic fiscal responsibility of adhering to a budget plan. Bureaucrats continue to overspend for reasons including deficient planning, political cronyism, and near-term gratification (i.e., votes). Some politicians believe that the ends justify the means (in other words, more public services justify more over-budget spending); however, the bigger picture shows that the means have become dauntingly costly. Even while liberals demand more tax increases (especially on higher earners), excessive borrowing practices from countries like China and Japan have contributed to racking up more than $18 trillion in U.S. debt.[10] This equates to roughly $58,000 of debt per citizen. With these amounts of money owed (and counting), we do not understand how any politician could rationally justify these ends.

The bipartisan Congressional Budget Office publishes an annual wasteful spending report highlighting publicly funded initiatives which have elements of excessive or unnecessary funding. For example, some government-funded operations seem to be little more than vote-buying opportunities disguised as social programs. Ironically, in spite of an endless supply of government bureaucracy, there is no department tasked with overseeing implementation of the CBO's findings. But beyond our interest in cutting unnecessary spending, we want to structurally reform the bureaucratic inefficiencies of government fiscal practices. Conservatives want to see government officials handle "other peoples' money" as responsibly as they handle their own (or at least as we would hope to be the case). A simple online search for "wasteful government spending" will produce results that may sound like exaggerated right-wing conspiracies, but sadly they are not. Politicians on both sides of the aisle are guilty of overspending and inefficiently spending taxpayers' money. A major difference is that conservativism is known to prioritize identifying and denouncing these reckless fiscal practices.

Liberals seem less alarmed by the government's wasteful spending habits. They are relatively less bothered by fiscal "details" as long as funding is made available to increase entitlements and address social matters. And when current funding proves ineffective, that is, when social and economic issues remain disappointingly stagnant, liberals call for increased spending

---

[10]   http://www.usgovernmentdebt.us/

funded by increased borrowing and tax rates on higher earners. Conservatives would be more inclined to agree to increased taxes, borrowing, or spending if evidence indicated that more money would in fact lead to a solution (see Taxes section). However, viable solutions do not result from the continued reckless practice of simply allocating more money to a problem.

Big government does not show signs of prioritizing ideas to streamline inefficient spending or rein in overwhelming debt. It continues to collect more in taxes from American individuals and businesses, as well as borrow more money from foreign countries and from Americans through the issuance of government bonds. Conservatives worry about the debt load on younger generations who will be burdened due to irresponsible spending and borrowing today. While we are not quite on the path of Greece, we should heed the warnings from such fiscally reckless, failing economies.

> Neither experience nor economic theory clearly indicates the threshold at which government debt begins to endanger prosperity and economic stability. But given the significant costs and risks associated with a rapidly rising federal debt, our nation should soon put in place a credible plan for reducing deficits to sustainable levels over time. — Ben Bernanke[11]

Conservatives are strong believers in fiscal responsibility in all aspects, private and public. We hold ourselves and we hold our government to the belief that we should live within our means — in other words, spend responsibly and operate with a sense

---

[11]   http://www.federalreserve.gov/newsevents/speech/
        bernanke20100427a.pdf

of priorities, limits, and sacrifice. The idea of fiscal responsibility recognizes that financial resources are finite (in other words, the taxpayers' wallets, like your personal wallet, are not bottomless wells) and therefore allocates spending based on the dollar amount budgeted. The practice of prioritizing "needs" and then "wants" to pay for goods, services, and investments is critical to responsible budgeting. On the other hand, fiscal irresponsibility, not uncommon in many bureaucracies, is demonstrated by carelessly spending in excess of dollars available and establishing debt that would be very difficult or impossible to repay (e.g., Greece, Portugal, Puerto Rico). We do not want our economy to continue on an irresponsible path given the severe fiscal and social burdens it places on every individual.

Labor

Conservatives believe that workers are the backbone of American society, as workers support themselves, their families, and their communities. Conservatives are often inaccurately viewed as supporting policies which are disadvantageous to the American worker and in favor of corporate big business. However, just like the other seemingly dichotomous political issues, labor policy is actually not that: policies which help the employer are not inevitably to the disadvantage of the employee; in kind, policies which help the employee are not automatically to the disadvantage of the employer. Supporting businesses and business owners is not our scheme for votes or donations from the "1%" (which based on numbers alone would clearly be a terrible strategy within a majority-rules democracy). Rather, we view our support of business (big and small) as a proxy for support of job creation. Jobs provide workers with a means of financial stability and an opportunity to further prosper. These jobs are held by workers who earn a living for themselves and their families, and meaningfully contribute to a productive society. Our labor policies do not aim to divide by employment class, but rather they aim to support the aggregate population.

Unions

Liberal Accusation: You do not support workers' rights.

BHC Counter: I support the rights of everyone, including the worker and the employer. I understand that at times the worker may feel overpowered (and may very well be overpowered) by a larger corporate entity. This is the reason I support initiatives, including laws and incentives, which recognize and protect workers' rights. While current labor laws have tremendously improved circumstances for workers, it may at times require an organization (that is, a unified voice) to oversee compliance of these laws by employers. So while I understand the benefits of specific labor union activity, I do not necessarily view the activities and initiatives of today's labor unions as protecting workers' rights; rather, I can understand how unions distort productivity and job opportunities. This dynamic actually hurts workers in the long run and therefore I believe labor union power ought to be kept in check.

There is a point at which the benefit of a labor union wanes. Typically, this point is reached when the union becomes too powerful and fails to consider the good of the company as well as the good of the member in its negotiations. That said, we do not view all union activity in a negative light. We recognize, for example, that without a union and in the absence of a benevolent employer, it is possible for an individual worker, subject to the whim of the employer, to be quite powerless. Contrary to the thinking of pure free market proponents, practicality and circumstance may prevent a worker from just quitting. Of course, there is no law preventing a dissatisfied worker from quitting an abusive work environment, however circumstances may. Those circumstances may include situations in which critically necessary medical insurance is tied to employment, or family support is dependent on steady income. While conservatives generally stand by free market principles, we also stand by personal fiscal responsibility — in some labor-related cases, we can see how a purely free market can conflict with the individual's objective of fiscal responsibility.

Conservatives support workers because they/we are the backbone of society. The goods and services produced by workers result in the growth and productivity which contribute to a flourishing economy. Conservatives equally support business owners primarily for the job opportunities they create for workers and society. Some labor unions, on the other hand, view the interests of workers and business owners as mutually exclusive. Being paid to unconditionally take the side of the workers, they may exude an unhealthy "us versus them" attitude toward the employer. We believe that some labor unions today actually perform a disservice to the workforce and the larger economy under the guise of protecting a helpless victimized worker from greedy exploitative business owners. This is a propagandized antiquated portrayal from times before workers' rights laws were passed.

In the mid-1800s, labor unions were a necessary response to the Industrial Revolution, when workplace health and mortality rates were real problems for workers.[12] Since that time, the U.S. has made tremendous progress on matters concerning workers' rights. Government organizations such as the Occupational Safety and Health Administration (OSHA) establish workers' rights laws. Conservatives recognize the significance of such legal measures and we support further private sector efforts. For instance, human resource departments are tasked to ensure compliance with worker protections such as OSHA and anti-discrimination laws. Although HR is a department within the corporate structure, arguably positioned in a conflict of interest, the availability of such resources for workers has contributed to the reduced urgency for workers to feel compelled to seek union representation. Today, union membership has dwindled as Americans understand that the workplace is legally required to be a safe place and free market employment competition influences fair labor practices.

Still, labor unions continue to claim to protect workers by defending their rights, primarily through efforts known as collective bargaining, as well as striking in worst case scenarios. They do this in exchange for union membership fees, ironically making the labor union a business unto itself. In many cases a worker employed by a business that is contracted to labor union terms is obligated to join the union, and joining requires union fees. Therefore, if the worker is not willing to pay for union representation then he or she is prohibited from employment by that business. The exception to this wayward rule lies in states with "right-to-work" laws which counteract the unfavorable influences of unions. In these states (currently

---

[12]   http://www.pbs.org/opb/historydetectives/feature/the-early-labor-movement/

25[13]), labor union powers are significantly curbed and there is no requirement for workers to join a union against their will. Conservatives support right-to-work laws. As then-Senator Barry Goldwater stated:

> Unions can be an instrument for achieving economic justice for the working man. Moreover, they are an alternative to, and thus discourage State Socialism. Most important they are an expression of freedom... But note that this function is perverted the moment a union claims the right to represent employees who do not want representation, or conducts activities that have nothing to do with terms of employment (e.g., political activities), or tries to deal with an industry as a whole instead of with individual employers. — Barry Goldwater[14]

Given today's circumstances and realities, present-day unions can be and have posed an unnecessary disruption within businesses as well as the general workforce. For example, teachers' unions often fight for public school teachers' job security regardless of teacher performance. As a result, it is extremely difficult for a union teacher to be fired regardless of failing job performance. In this case, as in many others involving short-sighted union ideals, union contract terms overpower goal-oriented job performance. Consequently, qualified educators looking to find their first teaching job have a tougher time finding employment — the supply of job opportunities is artificially lowered to favor unionized, tenured teachers who

---

13   http://www.nrtw.org/b/rtw_faq.htm
14   http://www.amazon.com/s/ref=nb_sb_noss?url=search-alias%3Dstripbooks&field-keywords=Conscience+of+a+Conservative+cc+goldwater

unconditionally remain so until they decide to quit on their own terms. As a result, the possibility exists that public school students, also subject to the terms of a teachers' union, may have no choice but to be assigned to a sub-standard teacher. This is a major reason for our support of non-unionized charter schools and teaching staff, as they are free to work unaffected by what could result in union-engendered conflicts of interest (see Education section).

A corporation and its employees can both be dragged down by what could sometimes become larger-scale negative effects resulting from the self-interest of some labor unions. For example, failed union labor negotiations contributed to the demise of the original Hostess, the maker of the iconic Twinkie. As the beleaguered baking company was figuring out how to keep the company afloat, union leaders and management could not come to an agreement on worker contract terms, resulting in a standoff which ended with 18,000 people out of work. The Hostess closing represents the irreparable damage unions can inflict on a company, but more importantly on thousands of individual workers and their families.

Wages

Liberal Accusation: You do not support a reasonable minimum wage for workers.

BHC Counter: I believe that a minimum wage floor should be legally set to ensure workers are not exploited. I also believe that minimum wage salary is intended to be an introductory income level for new or inexperienced workers with little or no skill set. In my view, policymakers should also consider varied minimum wages depending on, for instance, a municipality's cost of living. Overall I believe it is most appropriate for state or local level government to responsibly set a minimum wage amount which is reasonable for the worker as well as the employer. I understand that forcing an employer to pay its employees higher wages may come with unintended consequences, such as employee lay-offs which often leave minimum wage workers to be hit hardest.

As the wage debate more popularly relates to liberals calling for a federally mandated "living wage" (i.e., an amount high enough to support a basic standard of living), conservatives believe a minimum wage requirement based on this "standard" (which is not really standardized at all) is unmeritocratic and impractical. For example, enforcing a minimum wage fixed to an amount sufficient to support independent living is arbitrary. The many variables needing to be addressed include the cost of living in a given town, as well as the number of dependents (if any) supported by the worker. More practically speaking, a *federally* mandated inflated minimum wage is damaging to the broader job market and poses unintended consequences for the overall economy — negatively impacting all people, including workers.

The federal minimum wage is currently $7.25 per hour, though depending on state laws it can be a few dollars higher.[15] If the minimum wage is abruptly raised (many protesters call for hikes of more than 100%, alliteratively labeling their movement "Fight for $15"[16]), significant payroll costs would have negative repercussions on multiple levels, including the minimum wage worker. Contrary to liberal assumption, our sympathy on this

---

[15]   http://www.ncsl.org/research/labor-and-employment/state-minimum-wage-chart.aspx

[16]   http://nypost.com/2016/03/12/how-the-15-wage-is-already-killing-seattle-jobs/

matter is not with business. We realize that business owners could simply raise prices of goods and services to offset the financial impact of increased wages. This in turn would require customers to pay more out of their wallets. Put another way, through economically baseless federal minimum wage hikes, workers may receive more in paychecks; however, after their work day ends, they may spend more as consumers of goods and services. A resulting domino effect of increased salaries (including all the way up the workforce ladder) increases costs of goods and ultimately counteracts the intended purpose of the minimum wage hike (i.e., more unintended consequences). Increased income is redirected to fund increased expenses, virtually making that once-coveted "living wage" amount obsolete. Ultimately, it is possible that business owners may find it necessary to downsize, laying off some workers to offset increased overall payroll costs. This leaves fewer workers (albeit at higher wages) to "pick up the slack."

The liberal "living wage" position argues that the minimum wage should be set to an amount which at least puts a worker above the poverty line. This threshold set by the U.S. Census Bureau can range from $12,000 to $52,000 annually contingent upon a household's number of dependents.[17] While it sounds like a moral policy in a headline, making our alternative stance seem heartless, the reality is that passing this kind of wage law would be a gross misuse of resources and legislation. If the concern is truly focused on bringing a family out of poverty (which it absolutely is for conservatives), a federal minimum wage hike campaign may bring some votes to a liberal politician but it will not bring viable economic support to a struggling family. The way to sustainably fight poverty is by increasing quality job and

---

[17]   https://www.census.gov/hhes/www/poverty/data/threshld/

advancement opportunities, not by offering a few more dollars to achieve what results in the status quo.

Conservatives want to enact sustainable solutions to poverty and stagnant wages. Given our overarching support of an individual's freedom to choose, we believe government is not fit to mandate its "solutions" on private businesses. Rather, government could help with this endeavor through creating incentives for employers to enrich and empower their employees. For example, corporate tax breaks for companies demonstrating a legitimized standard of employee raises or low turnover is a conservative-style strategy. We believe that hard-working employees should have the opportunity to earn financial stability and pursue upward mobility. Similarly, we believe job-producing businesses should have the opportunity to attract workers in a sustainable manner. We commend businesses which are able and willing to offer better pay and promote their workers.

Income Inequality

Liberal Accusation: You are callously indifferent to the injustices of income inequality.

BHC Counter: I am very concerned by a lack of economic opportunities available to those of lower socioeconomic status. This lack of opportunity is what unfortunately causes the income of many workers to be unacceptably low. The comparison to higher income earners is irrelevant, making *income* inequality, yet another alarming alliteration generated by liberals, not actually the problem. Rather, *opportunity* inequality is the problem needing to be addressed to help solve the socioeconomic struggles of so many Americans. I believe the solution exists in opening up opportunities for these citizens (often in the form of government deregulation). Most notably, strategies to improve education and to grow job prospects can increase incomes and in turn bring comfortable, stable lives with continued opportunities for advancement. I am eager to elevate the lower and middle classes, which should and can only effectively be done by recognizing the fallacy of liberal policies vilifying and penalizing higher earners:

> Governments need to keep their focus on pushing up the bottom and middle rather than dragging down the top: investing in (and removing barriers to) education, abolishing rules that prevent the able from getting ahead and refocusing government spending on those that need it most.[18]

Poverty and working class struggles, the literal problems of this debate, concern both conservatives and liberals. We both have ideas on how to solve these problems, but we differ in what we see as the cause and therefore the solution to these problems. From the liberal perspective, the cause is income inequality — the income gap between higher earners and lower earners. They believe that high incomes of wealthier individuals come at the expense of the middle and lower classes. As a result, their solution is redistribution of wealth. This is commonly exemplified by taxing upper income earners at much higher rates in order to pass that money — in the form of government-allotted subsidies and entitlements — to lower income earners. From the conservative perspective, a gap between higher income earners and lower income earners has no bearing on the cause or solution to the issue. Rather,

---

[18]   http://www.economist.com/node/17959590

the cause is opportunity inequality (also a problem in and of itself) — hurdles inhibiting equal economic opportunities for lower socioeconomic classes. Accordingly, our solutions revolve around removing barriers in the way of accessing tools for self-empowerment and opportunities to pursue upward mobility.

Contrary to the liberal perspective focused on income inequality, the economic achievement of some does not come at the expense of the middle and lower class (see Capitalism section). Therefore, we do not believe taking more and more taxes from financially successful Americans in the name of achieving income *equality* is beneficial to lower income earners — and we have seen in practice that this is not a favorable strategy for anyone. As it stands today, the top 20% of earners pay more than 80% of total income tax collected by the federal government, and the top 1% pay nearly 50% of total income tax.[19] In the meantime, poverty rates and welfare recipients have only increased over the past decade.[20] [21] If government-run public anti-poverty programs cannot be effective with more than 80% of the government's wallet funded by 20% of its citizens, then we are highly skeptical (put mildly) that more of the same government tax policy will improve the status quo for the lower class.

We recognize that income *equality*, an ideal in line with that of socialism, comes at the expense of personal economic freedoms and mobility. However, in the U.S., where economic freedoms

---

[19] http://www.wsj.com/articles/top-20-of-earners-pay-84-of-income-tax-1428674384

[20] https://www.census.gov/hhes/www/poverty/data/historical/people.html

[21] http://www.cato.org/blog/years-after-recession-welfare-rolls-hit-new-highs

and mobility are prized basic rights, we are free to pursue different kinds of education, professions in various industries, entrepreneurial risks, and personal financial decisions as we see fit. The level of preparation and effort, among many other variables, associated with each personal endeavor typically influences personal income, causing income levels to vary accordingly. From this sense, where freedom and individuality exist, unequal incomes are a natural result of pursuing diverse opportunities. Poverty and opportunity inequality, on the other hand, are separate matters which are not viably resolved through socialist-based redistribution policies, as supported by many liberals. Such policies are erroneously grounded in the belief that higher-income earners gain at the expense of lower-income earners. In other words, the U.S. economy is not a zero-sum game (see Capitalism section). Enforcing this kind of policy would restrain the breadth of all Americans' freedoms, preferences, and potentials.

With our focus on improving opportunity equality, we can solve the root problem: poverty and a struggling working class. Our philosophical theme of equal opportunity for all insists that every American regardless of background should have the opportunity to pursue upward mobility, financial stability, and general prosperity — that is the American dream. While conservatives understand how a free market system paves the path to that American dream, we also realize there are at times socioeconomic obstacles along this path. We look to promote and enhance factors which equip individuals with the resources to overcome challenges which stand in the way of opportunity. The kinds of policies which enable better job creation, job training, and education will fundamentally improve income potential for individuals of underprivileged backgrounds. We view our approach as the way to *sustainably* solve the problem.

Through conservative-minded strategies which focus on the fundamentals (rather than on an income redistribution blame-game distracting attention away from the problem), the U.S. stays true to the values of economic freedom for the individual and equal opportunity for all.

Social Security

Liberal Accusation: You want to cut the Social Security safety net for senior citizens and retirees.

BHC Counter: I believe current and future senior citizens who have paid into the Social Security system during working years deserve to be supported during elderly years. However, the source of support, the Social Security fund, has long been running a deficit with no end in sight. The government needs to prioritize Social Security reform — perhaps, for example, involving eligibility age changes and/or some transition to private sector management. If the government continues to procrastinate or make empty promises around reform, then a drastic emergency "solution" (which is likely no real solution) will be the only option available for a problem too significant for such negligence.

Conservatives want to reform the Social Security system to preserve its intended goals — to provide income to senior citizens during their retirement years. Because the system's problems have become so mired in deficits due to fiscally irresponsible government planning (a sadly reoccurring theme), we understand that honest reform will not be a seamless transition. "Duct-taping" a temporary solution which might ingratiate short-sighted voters would ultimately burden future generations. We realize the responsible action is to make some sacrifices now for sustainable reform. Contrary to liberal accusation, this does not imply that we want to eliminate the system — but we do have to reconstruct the system. The country's demographic makeup has changed so drastically since the inception of the system that its plans and assumptions have not been able to keep up with the shifts — understanding these circumstances is critical to reform.

The Social Security problem stems from an outdated government-sponsored retirement safety net model legislated in very different times, under very different circumstance. The U.S. Social Security Act was passed in 1935, when life expectancy was less than 62 years and roughly 8 million Americans were 65 years and older.[22][23] At that time the worker-to-SS beneficiary ratio was 15:1.[24] Fast forward to 2012, roughly one lifetime from SS enactment: life expectancy has increased to 79 years, and 43 million Americans are 65 years and older;[25][26] that is five times the population from when the system was planned. The worker-to-SS beneficiary ratio has decreased drastically to roughly 3:1.[27] With life expectancy continuing to increase and birth rates at all-time lows,[28] it is clear that there will not be enough taxable young earners to sustainably support the number of elderly citizens. Given the way the Social

---

[22] http://www.cdc.gov/nchs/data/nvsr/nvsr63/nvsr63_07.pdf

[23] https://www.census.gov/content/dam/Census/library/
      publications/2014/demo/p23-212.pdf

[24] http://www.nolo.com/legal-encyclopedia/social-security-benefits-
      retirement-32416.html

[25] http://www.cdc.gov/nchs/data/hus/hus14.pdf#015

[26] http://www.census.gov/prod/2014pubs/p25-1140.pdf

[27] http://www.nolo.com/legal-encyclopedia/social-security-benefits-
      retirement-32416.html

[28] http://www.livescience.com/48995-us-birth-rate-hits-all-time-low.html

Security system is currently (or rather archaically) designed, the increase in longevity is especially exacerbating the issue — roughly 15 more years in lifespan means 15 more years of social security payments. Multiplying this by an estimated 56 million retirees in 2020 and then 80 million retirees in 2040[29] makes for an avalanche of payments not considered when the Social Security Act was signed (pre-Baby Boomer era) in 1935. In short, the decline in birth rates, retirement of the Baby Boomer generation, and increase in life expectancy present a perfect storm for the future of Social Security, particularly for workers currently paying into the system but not expecting to receive much in return upon retirement.[30]

Our federal government started running deficits on Social Security in 2010. At that point, the government began paying out more money in SS benefits than it was taking in via payroll taxes.[31] If we delay reforming the current deficit-ridden SS model, the inevitable consequence will be that we are forced to involve some combination of: 1) a significant increase in minimum eligibility age; 2) a drastic increase in SS tax rates on workers; 3) a considerable decrease in SS check amounts to levels scarcely subsidizing elderly living. A graduated implementation of some of these variables has been discussed as a possible solution and some incremental actions have already been taken, but not to the degree which truly staves off the unavoidable problem. We want to prioritize SS reform so we may meet the problem with solutions rather than be dumped on with consequences. There is generally bipartisan

29   http://www.census.gov/prod/2014pubs/p25-1140.pdf
30   http://www.gallup.com/poll/184580/americans-doubt-social-security-benefits.aspx
31   http://www.nolo.com/legal-encyclopedia/social-security-benefits-retirement-32416.html

agreement that something must be done, but the political frustrations come with how, where, and when is the right way to reform. Conservatives, relative to liberals, are more proactive with regard to our priority of solving the SS issue — which is ironic given the false pop-politicized stereotype that we are the party callous to social causes.

One example of a conservative-style approach to help rectify the SS system would call for automatic IRAs implemented by employers to serve as a personalized SS fund in place of, or in tandem with, the government-run SS system (note, this is another government-run public institution demonstrating ineptitude). Payroll deductions could be invested in financial markets (e.g., bond funds and dividend-paying equity funds) of appropriate risk-reward profiles, depending on, for instance, the age of the individual. This would facilitate and simplify personal savings so the individual private citizen, not the government, can be more in direct control of his or her finances and retired livelihood. Liberals, however, are averse to the idea of letting financial markets influence the funds of a safety net program. Ironically, they are also critical of the wealth built by those who invest in financial markets. We view this approach as one which preserves the goal of the safety net style system while implementing elements of independence and choice.

PART III
SOCIAL

Social Issues with Fiscal Significance

In the so-called binary world of domestic politics, issues are categorized as either social or fiscal. Often what constitutes a conservative is the understanding that many characteristically social issues actually have considerable fiscal implications. These fiscally-social issues are not necessarily about capitalism, economics, or government spending. Rather, they are about understanding the kinds of social policies which appropriately incentivize optimal fiscal behavior, particularly for those who need financial support or protection. These considerations are mentioned in each section where relevant but the immediate sections to follow are frequently misrepresented as purely social matters. Conservatives recognize that social and fiscal matters are not mutually exclusive. In fact, wise fiscal policies can make for the most supportive and compassionate social policies.

Welfare

Liberal Accusation: You do not support welfare.

BHC Counter: I think that providing welfare benefits is one of the most important responsibilities of government. The liberal-drawn caricature that Republicans believe solely in free market capitalism and oppose welfare is absurd, largely because we understand that one cannot exist without the other. For a dispassionate and academic perspective on this matter, consider economist Richard McKenzie, who argues, "The welfare state is not only desirable but most likely necessary for the continued collective acceptance of the market system."[1] His point is that it is inevitable that workers will be displaced from time to time in a free market. Without government assistance during those hard times, workers would impede free markets, resulting in a greater cost to growth than the cost of welfare.

But my belief in the importance of welfare does not come from the cold ivory towers of academia. I am a *bleeding heart* conservative after all! I would like to see more dollars go to the programs that most effectively help the truly needy. When someone falls on hard times, government aid acts as a safety net. As we see it, liberals prefer to cast a much wider and less scrutinized safety net than that of conservatives. A wider safety net is a less selective net, catching those who are not in sincere need of aid or who "need" it due to lack of personal effort to find work. The reality is that a less selective safety net, for example one which does not require work or work-related activities,[2] acts as a disincentive for some physically and mentally capable yet unmotivated people to work. As a result, they take shares of benefits away from those who truly need meaningful help.

---

1   http://www.amazon.com/The-Fairness-Markets-Justice-Society/dp/0669148016

2   https://www.washingtonpost.com/opinions/how-obama-has-gutted-welfore-reform/2012/09/06/885b0092-f835-11e1-8b93-c4f4ab1c8d13_story.html

This is not only an illegitimate exploitation of the system, but also an immoral exploitation of welfare recipients truly in need. Ultimately, conservatives want to be able to provide more to those who need help to get back on their feet.

A liberal welfare system lacks an appropriate level of accountability, as shown by a disturbing rate of erroneous uses of safety net funds[3] as well as an unacceptable status quo of high joblessness, poverty, and hunger rates. The absence of governmental accountability has compromised the true intent of welfare support: "The original purpose of the welfare state was to lift people into self-sufficiency, not to create a permanent underclass dependent on taxpayers. Lyndon Johnson told us when he started these programs that 'the days of the dole are numbered.' We have passed day 18,000."[4] Conservatives are in favor of EBT cards (i.e., food stamps), but not when such programs lack the administrative accountability to prevent questionable purchases — cigarettes, alcohol, gambling — which are damaging to a recipient's well-being or return to self-sufficiency. Only recently was it required that "all states must prevent the use of cash benefits in liquor stores, gambling establishments and adult entertainment businesses by 2014. States that fail to establish policies face cuts in federal support."[5] This law passed because blatant abuse of government aid is an unfortunate reality; for example, reports of "people with welfare

---

3   http://waysandmeans.house.gov/boustany-opening-statement-protecting-the-safety-net-from-waste-fraud-and-abuse/

4   http://dailysignal.com/2015/05/18/unraveling-the-poverty-myths-obama-is-promoting/

5   http://usatoday30.usatoday.com/news/nation/story/2012-07-08/welfare-purchase-restrictions/56100508/1

debit cards withdrawing thousands of dollars from ATMs in casinos, liquor stores, and strip clubs." This is not to suggest that any significant portion of welfare recipients abuse the system. Rather, our contention here, aside from our principled stance against unaccountable government bureaucracy, is that abuse and fraud result in resources, in one form or another, being taken from those who genuinely need and use welfare support as a bridge to independence. In addition to increased scrutiny on welfare purchases, conservatives support stringent work and training requirements for able-minded, able-bodied welfare recipients. Essentially, we want the welfare system to be "a reciprocal relationship between the taxpayer and welfare recipient... to convey expectations that public assistance is temporary [as it's] directed towards restoring self-sufficiency."[6]

Conservatives want to streamline the welfare system not solely for morality or accountability, but also to make funds available for proactively impactful public programs. Welfare dollars saved from illegitimate uses could be redirected to make more funding available for need-based, self-empowerment initiatives such as education focused on vocational skills, job training, or personal savings management. As a result, the number of welfare applicants and rate of recurrence would decrease. President Reagan put it best when he said, "We should measure welfare's success by how many people leave welfare, not by how many were added."[7] A more targeted and responsible distribution of welfare dollars would help achieve

---

6   http://dailysignal.com/2015/02/04/20-children-food-stamps-heres-change/

7   http://townhall.com/columnists/robertknight/2014/02/05/welfare-reform-n1787955/page/full

that success for the individual as well as for the long-term solvency of the system. In *The Conservative Heart*, author Arthur Brooks notes that Reagan "recognized the moral truth that a real social safety net is one of the great achievements of our free market system." And Brooks explains that because "fiscal profligacy actually poses a massive threat to the social safety net... we must protect it with fiscal discipline. There is no other way."[8]

Finally, we believe welfare support is most wisely allocated and distributed at the most local level possible. State and local governments are inherently most in tune and in touch with the needs of their communities. The federal government, on the other hand — comprised of politicians sitting in D.C. with likely skewed understanding (or for that matter interest) — is not the most efficient arbiter of what has become an ineffectual $746 billion annual welfare program. Given unmistakable misallocations of resources as well as the more than 80 overlapping programs under the federal welfare structure,[9] we want to reform and localize the welfare system so Americans in need of help can receive appropriate support in order to ultimately be self-reliant and prosper.

Health Care

Liberal Accusation: You do not believe the government should provide health care to its citizens.

---

[8]   http://www.washingtontimes.com/news/2015/jul/15/book-review-the-conservative-heart-how-to-build-a-/?page=all

[9]   http://www.budget.senate.gov/republican/public/index.cfm/files/serve/?File_id=34919307-6286-47ab-b114-2fd5bcedfeb5

BHC Counter: Similar to my belief in welfare (see Welfare section), I believe that the government should provide health care access to those in need and who cannot sufficiently provide for themselves. Since 1965 Medicaid and Medicare have provided this health care safety net to Americans in need of assistance due to lack of finances, disability, or old age. But as seen in many government-run programs, notably the recently exposed scandals and mishandling of patients at the Veterans Health Administration, bureaucracy and inefficiency do not inspire confidence in depending on federal management (e.g., the Affordable Care Act) to solve health care issues, nor to improve the overall industry. Beyond addressing the specific concern for poor citizens in need, I generally believe a robust and efficient health care industry (for both the patient and provider) is created with *limited* government intervention.

Well before the introduction of the purely Democrat-endorsed Affordable Care Act (ACA; also known as Obamacare), we have been aware of and concerned with the flaws in our health care industry — notably costs. The costs of health care have risen disproportionately for a number of reasons, ranging from economic challenges to demographic shifts to policy regulations (some reasonable, some not[10]). While Democrats claim the ACA will improve industry costs, many independent experts forecast that it "won't stop the cost of health care from continuing to rise and consumers from paying bigger bills."[11] Hospital, physician, and clinical care costs — the major factors impacting annual health care expenditures — continue to be driven up in part due to rising costs of labor, goods, and

---

[10]   http://www.ncbi.nlm.nih.gov/pmc/articles/PMC2730786/

[11]   http://money.cnn.com/2012/07/12/news/economy/health-care-costs/

services. Other factors include increasing demand for care and compliance with regulatory requirements. The ACA's new laws imposing more industry regulations and administrative expenses are just a few of the bureaucracies which will exacerbate health care costs for providers — to pass on to the patient in the form of higher bills.

The economic factors affecting the health care industry are comparable to many factors impacting other industries. Like other industries, a fiscally-conservative free market approach (with some regulation largely in the form of incentives and disincentives) would control for *unreasonable* cost increases. In a free market, health care insurance companies would be free to compete for patient coverage across state lines — in other words, to acquire customers nationwide by offering a combination of better quality and controlled cost. Unfortunately, a free market scenario is not the reality for health care — and the ACA virtually federally institutionalizes the industry. In part, as a result of increased government regulations overpowering free market dynamics, we see health care experiencing disproportionate growth in costs. Redistributing financial responsibility from patients who do not pay or do not fully pay to individuals and their insurers or to the government covering Medicare/Medicaid bills (which counts for 60% of all hospital admissions) ultimately distorts costs.

Americans unqualified for Medicaid generally fit one of two scenarios: pay reasonable-to-inflated amounts for health care through insurance, or forgo health care coverage altogether because insurance is not worth the financial cost. In either scenario, we believe health care is very important — too important to be held hostage with inflated costs or forgoing coverage — so we know that industry reform is needed. We also know that government-managed health care as mandated in the ACA is not reform; rather, we see it as expanded Medicaid. As already demonstrated by federal programs like Medicaid and the VA, a government solution to health care industry issues will decrease availability of quality health care and increase cost of health care for many. The ACA's financial burdens on the consumer have only begun to come to fruition, as "health insurance experts are predicting that premiums will rise more significantly in 2016 than in the first two years of Obamacare exchange coverage. In 2015, premiums increased by an average of 5.4 percent." [12] As for the availability of quality coverage, many patients (at least 3.5 million and counting) have been dropped by their existing insurance plans and/or their existing doctors since the implementation of the ACA.[13] These people are left with little choice but to pay for a more expensive individual plan to keep their doctors or find other doctors willing to take them under a sub-optimal ACA public exchange plan.[14]

The ACA's impact on health care cost and quality is also largely a result of the Act's impositions on private enterprises of business owners, doctors' practices, and the health insurance industry. The ACA's increased insurance requirements for businesses with more than 50 full-time employees incentivizes

12   http://www.politico.com/story/2015/05/how-affordable-is-the-affordable-care-act-118428
13   http://www.businessinsider.com/at-least-35-million-americans-have-now-had-their-health-insurance-policies-canceled-thanks-to-obamacare-2013-11
14   http://www.cnn.com/2013/12/18/politics/obamacare-insurers-dumping-doctors/

many employers, in particular small business owners without the scale to bear ACA burdens, to cut workers' hours and reduce full-time head-count to less than 50. Along those lines, this also discourages employers from expanding their workforce beyond 50 full-time employees to avoid passing the threshold which would require fulfilling an ACA mandate to provide health insurance — just some of the unintended consequences of the ACA. Private medical practices are also now under more government regulations. The increase in compliance logistics and subsequent changes in insurance fee structures (i.e., compensation to physicians) have caused many physicians to opt out of accepting certain kinds of insurance or any insurance at all. As observed by the president of the Medical Society of the State of New York, "The [ACA] exchanges have become very much like Medicaid... Physicians who are in solo practices have to be careful not to take too many patients reimbursed at lower rates or they're not going to be in business very long."[15] We realize that physicians entered their profession for many reasons, including a love of medicine, helping the sick, and financial reward. Unlikely to be on this list is to work under federal bureaucratic oversight. Furthermore, becoming a physician is not inexpensive or easy so we especially want to maintain, and to the extent possible improve, incentives (financial and otherwise) for those wanting to pursue a medical profession.

As for the ACA's effect on the insurance industry, private insurers have changed or altogether canceled policies since the Act's implementation. Limiting coverage and increasing expenses to the covered patient are some ways insurers have

---

[15]   http://www.usatoday.com/story/news/nation/2014/10/27/insurers-aca-exchange-plans-lower-reimbursements-doctors/17747839/

tried to manage regulatory burdens and offset unfavorable terms now mandated by the federal government.[16] [17] As it relates to the ACA's public insurance marketplace, a limited number of coverage options essentially offer a "one-size-fits-all" insurance plan. This means that everyone under a given ACA plan has little choice but to pay for certain coverages which could never apply to them; for example, a childless couple in their 60s paying for pediatric coverage.[18] The government's proclivity for inefficient use of resources has become cliché — the ACA further demonstrates this. With specific regard to the ACA's full birth control coverage, we argue that government does not have the right to require others to pay for a person's sexual recreation (see Contraception section). However, we understand that affordable birth control has come to be a culturally practical matter.

Beyond the inefficient and inconvenient economics of the ACA, conservatives believe the Act is an unconstitutional overstep of government in that it requires its citizens to purchase health insurance or face penalties for noncompliance. While we are inclined to believe that purchasing insurance is typically a wise, responsible decision (after all, our political namesake, "conservative", implies caution and hedging), we do not believe that citizens should be federally obligated to pay for anything except taxes (creatively, some then argue the ACA is a tax by

---

16   http://www.usatoday.com/story/opinion/2014/10/16/obama-health-care-insurance-cancellation-column/17353673/

17   http://www.nytimes.com/2014/11/15/us/politics/cost-of-coverage-under-affordable-care-act-to-increase-in-2015.html?_r=0

18   http://www.forbes.com/sites/mikepatton/2014/03/13/obamacare-charges-millions-of-unsuspecting-americans-for-coverage-theyll-never-use/

way of penalty for refusing to buy insurance[19]). Our nation was founded on a principle of individual freedom — outside the civic responsibility of paying taxes (not penalties in the form of taxes), individual freedom does not involve the government dictating logistics of personal health care or forcing the purchase of health insurance plans deemed appropriate by politicians.

Many Democrats argue that the government should make health care a fully public enterprise — truly comprehensive universal health care as practiced in some other countries. While we agree the idea of guaranteed health care for all sounds compassionate and humane, the inconvenient truth is that indiscriminate practice of it is not necessarily so. Proponents of universal health care tout the systems of societies like Singapore or Canada. What this argument does not take into account is that every country has its own set of characteristics, making a given health care system not necessarily applicable to another society — for example, Singapore's population of 5 million or Canada's 35 million versus the United States' 320 million citizens. Even with a fraction of our population size, these countries' socialized health care systems involve extraordinarily long wait times[20] for medically necessary treatment. Nevertheless, we do wish to study the systems of other countries and apply specific relevant insights where appropriate. For instance, Avik Roy of the Manhattan Institute, a center-right policy research think tank, recommends adopting specific lessons from Singapore and Switzerland. [21] In his policy paper, *Transcending Obamacare*, he

---

19   http://www.forbes.com/sites/beltway/2012/07/03/some-tax-few-will-face-obamacare-uninsured-penalty-and-irs-hamstrung-to-collect/

20   http://www.forbes.com/sites/theapothecary/2015/08/07/no-donald-trump-single-payer-health-care-doesnt-work-incredibly-well-in-canada-scotland/

21   http://www.manhattan-institute.org/html/mpr_17.htm#.Ve2oJxFViko

identifies effective means-tested support systems for the poor and uninsured and integrates them within a fiscally responsible, consumer-driven model.

Regardless of one's political view, it is tough to deny the reality that U.S. public institutions such as the post office, public schools, Medicaid, and the VA demonstrate underwhelming efficiency and quality — a characteristic not new or unique to government-run organizations. Therefore, we want to avoid handing over more of the health care industry to government mismanagement. The inevitable participation of industry lobbyists and special interest groups makes us even more averse (to the extent that's possible) to the idea. Ultimately we are most supportive of achieving a nationally competitive health care system. As conservatives, we understand how free market competition enables an individual's freedom to choose the most suitable insurance company while promoting high quality and reasonable cost. Sound safety net coverage to back any citizens in need would supplement such a system. Short of government takeover, we are open to left-leaning suggestions to help make that happen.

Tort Reform

Liberal Accusation: You do not support a victim's right to file suit in a court of law.

BHC Counter: I support any individual who truly believes he or she was harmed to seek appropriate recompense in a court of law. I believe that tort liability provides justice for the victim and for the rightly accused offender. Equally significant, tort liability serves as a form of disincentive for citizens who may otherwise interact or transact negligently. With this in mind, I also recognize that it is possible for the accused to actually be the victim in our overly litigious society. The consequences of this go beyond the individuals involved in a tort case. Societal behavior and increased industry legal costs (which, by the way, is passed on to the patient, customer, or consumer) are only a few of the unintended consequences of illegitimate tort allegations.

Regardless of political affiliation, many would agree that the frivolous lawsuit is an embarrassing practice in the U.S. "Frivolous," of course, is relative, which is what makes this issue complex. Some might file a tort lawsuit for a legitimate grievance, a technical fault, or an attempt to recoup easy money with little-to-no downside. While tort lawsuits may serve as a means for the "little guy" (e.g., the private individual) to have a voice against a larger dominant entity (e.g., big corporations, doctors), the fact is that individuals of all sizes and statures may look to take advantage of their right to file suits by falsely claiming victimhood. Those individuals, including private citizens and their tort lawyers (not so fondly known as "ambulance-chasers"), seek financial gain for themselves at the expense of the unreasonably accused and more broadly at the expense of society. Because of the unjust and far-reaching unintended consequences of what tort liability has become, conservatives want to reform the tort system. Ultimately we want those who do wrong to continue to be held accountable, but create disincentives for illegitimate litigants (i.e., accusers).

Contrary to liberal assumption, we do not want to dismantle the tort system to protect big corporations and leave the individual without protections. The case of *Pearson v. Chung* (below) illustrates how the current tort system is not about big versus little — it is about a litigious society gone awry given warped incentives, or insufficient disincentives. An overarching element of conservatism is the importance of incentives, and lawsuits act as an incentive for accountability and ethical procedure. In kind, we want disincentives in place to deter people from filing frivolous arguments and obviously false claims of damage, injury, or the ever-vague "mental distress." The case of *Pearson v. Chung* illustrates just that: Roy Pearson sued the Chung family's local dry cleaning business over a pair of pants he paid ($10.50) to be altered. The alteration was not finished on time and the returned pants were allegedly not his. The dispute found its way to court, where Pearson claimed he was entitled to compensation for damages involving emotional distress, legal fees, fraudulence, and 10 years' worth of weekend car rentals (for travel to a different dry cleaner) totaling more than $50 million. The Chung family offered a series of settlements, all denied by Pearson. As a result of the case, the family found themselves running through their savings in legal fees, harming their credit, and considering a move back to their native South Korea.[22] Ultimately the court ruled in favor of Chung. In our opinion however, given current tort law, justice was not completely served for the Chung family.

The consequences of "crying wolf" in the real world lead to increased costs in many areas affecting others' daily lives. The eagerness for some individuals to look for reasons to bring suit and some lawyers enabling this self-serving behavior contribute to a general cost inflation of many goods and services. In health care for example, doctors are subject to exorbitant malpractice insurance costs, which they naturally pass on to the patient — a factor contributing to the reasons U.S. health

---

22   http://www.wsj.com/articles/SB118212479726338524

care costs are unnecessarily high. While professionals of any industry should absolutely be held accountable for negligent or intentional missteps, the manner in which society ensures this accountability should be reasonable. Reasonably ensuring accountability may include reasonably avoiding or at least diminishing the domino effect of passing costs to unrelated parties. Conservative tort reform looks to counter the unreasonable aspects and unintended consequences of the tort system.

Given the intention of tort liability to keep people accountable for their actions, the tort system can elicit unintended consequences such as reluctance of "good Samaritans." Those who are aware of the overly litigious culture in the U.S. understand that involvement in another person's circumstance may imply liability in the event of an unfavorable outcome — resulting in otherwise good Samaritans to remain uninvolved bystanders. To counteract this regrettable social cost, some jurisdictions have enacted Good Samaritan Laws to protect people who try to help others. Unfortunately, the law does not apply in all states in all areas, leaving good Samaritans vulnerable to liability. This tort-induced legality is unfortunate for an individual in need of help and unfortunate for the overall culture of our society.

Conservatives wish to reform the tort system to maintain its legitimate intentions while counteracting illegitimate complaints which result in high financial and social costs, as well as a decline in respect for the system. We view the offenses of an illegitimate accuser (i.e., claimant) potentially as serious as the offenses of a legitimate offender (i.e., defendant). Some reform advocates propose measures such as placing procedural limits on filing certain claims, capping plaintiff awards, or placing responsibility on the claimant to subsidize a cleared defendant's legal and defamatory costs. With some degree of application of such measures, our society can hopefully ease the overly-litigious culture we unintentionally created.

Education

Conservatives view education as one of the most important functions of society, and we make the issue a priority among our many concerns. In addition to parental guidance and community support, education is the most effective way to enable self-reliance, instill self-discipline, and inspire self-empowerment. That emphasis on the "self" translates to independence, and the more independent an individual, the more he or she can do for himself or herself and, in turn, for society. We want to improve our public education system in tandem with allowing "free market"-style school choice (including public, charter, private, voucher) within the broader education system. The two goals of improving public schools and encouraging school choice are really one and the same. In a more competitive educational landscape with many schooling options, public schools will be motivated (or pressured) to no longer complacently rely on mediocre results (which has become the current reality for American students). Given a belief in the success which comes with free market principles, it is evident to us why the public education market is broken: public schools operate within a system distorted by government regulations and union terms which stifle healthy free market competition. If schools competed to earn student enrollment (and with that each student's allotted public tuition dollars) and had greater incentives to improve student outcomes, we would expect improvements in the quality of teaching, attendance rates, and test results, to name a few. These expected improvements are notwithstanding the outsized contribution enabled by the critical foundation of good parenting in all socioeconomic backgrounds. Beyond educational improvements by way of schools and teachers, other matters related to the success of our education system involve policies and practices which align with principles of equality and respect.

Schools

Liberal Accusation: You don't care about the failing public school system, particularly those which plague low-income minority communities.

BHC Counter: I care deeply about the health of our public school system, as well as our broader education system, which includes alternatives to public schools. I want every child of every socioeconomic background to have access to a proper education and healthy learning environment. Strong schools are especially important for students in disadvantaged communities who may lack the structure and resources at home to guide them away from trouble and lead them toward their studies.

In some areas around the country, traditional public schools succeed in educating and developing our children. However, in other areas, most often in underprivileged communities, public schools fail to sufficiently educate and engage students. The discrepancies are evidenced by test scores, grades, attendance rates, and drop-out rates. Unfortunately, from an overall standpoint, current public education policies have failed American students, as they slip in the rankings against global student test scores.[23] Liberals see this dismal phenomenon as justification for allocating more tax dollars to what we recognize as blatantly failed policies. For example, less than stellar public education districts like New York City and Baltimore are among the top five highest spending per pupil[24] — we do not see the logic leading some liberals to conclude that more spending implies improved education. In response to our understanding that more funding has not and will not fix failed public education policies, liberals blame us for neglecting minority students and acting against teachers. To the contrary, we absolutely want all students of all backgrounds, particularly those in at-risk communities, to access great schools and great teachers to prepare for a better future. The truth is that both conservatives and liberals want to improve the education system, but we have different ideas on how this can be achieved. Beyond the circumstance of the home environment and community — critical variables which ideally should lay the educational foundations of discipline and responsibility — we see ways within *and* supplementary to the public system to improve education opportunities for children of any background and circumstance.

Teachers' unions are an extremely influential force within our public education system. Similar to any union, the teachers' union focuses on the best interest of its members (see Unions section). This does not always coincide with the best interest of students, however. While the administrative burden on many teachers can become excessive, possibly at the cost of the student experience, we recognize that the overall influence

---

23   http://www.wsj.com/articles/SB100014240527023045794045792345
11824563116
24   https://www.census.gov/newsroom/press-releases/2015/cb15-98.
html

and power of the union needs to be kept in check. Teachers' unions can and do serve a useful purpose but this comes into question because of their mandate to defend and protect all teachers, including sub-standard teachers (often found in the infamous "rubber room"[25] or reassignment centers). Further, the general success of non-unionized charter schools and private schools demonstrate that excessively influential unions are unnecessary and may negatively impact the ultimate goal of motivating and educating students. While liberals unconditionally support teachers' unions, a strong voting bloc of the Democratic Party, we recognize both sides of the coin, so we want the education system and policies to strike the right balance.

Federal government intervention via D.C.-based Department of Education is another influential disruptive factor we view as characteristically disconnected from the educational interest of local students and their families. We believe an *excessive* level of government intervention, particularly from the federal government, is not ideal for any social or economic function; this is particularly true of our education system. In line with our general political philosophy, we view federal involvement here as inappropriate — with federal funding comes federal management, bureaucracies, and out-of-touch "conditions" (in other words, restrictions and requirements). Consequently, inevitable conflict manifests (knowingly and unintentionally) between D.C. influence and local realities. If the Feds can guarantee *no* external conditions tied to a particular appropriate funding need (e.g., disabilities education), then federal support

---

25   http://www.nydailynews.com/new-york/education/city-schools-
      rubber-rooms-bounce-back-article-1.1184406

in specific cases would be reasonable and valued. Generally speaking, however, we want state and local governments fully in charge of their communities' education, which requires excusing federal dealings from local education.

"There is no place where... an educational system can be better understood than locally, where a community has the opportunity to view and judge the product of its own school system,"[26] noted Barry Goldwater in *The Conscience of a Conservative*. We (not surprisingly) agree — educational agendas tailored and funded at local levels, where officials are in tune with the concerns and needs of its citizens, is the most effective approach. A locally run and managed education system is more efficient and more dynamic. Local control lends itself to more customizable solutions, including instructional approaches, charter schools, private schools (with need-based subsidies), and voucher systems. In the case of vouchers, parents have the freedom to choose their child's school (i.e., out-of-zone public, independent charter, or subsidized private). The voucher allows individuals to take their per-student allotment of public education money to a school of their choice, rather than being restricted to a school zone assigned by the government and partly administered by unions. Conservative-minded solutions like school vouchers empower freedom of choice, helping parents and students to access suitable education in a school system more closely resembling a free market.

Charter schools, an increasingly popular option for many parents and students (and conservatives!), have become

---

[26]   http://www.amazon.com/Conscience-Conservative-Madison-American-Politics/dp/0691131171/ref=sr_1_sc_1?s=books&ie=UTF8&qid=1442368762&sr=1-1-spell&keywords=cc+goldwter

a political hot topic as many charters have demonstrated sustainable success in the education market (to the dismay of public school teachers' unions). Charter schools are publicly funded, independently operated schools that are allowed to function with more autonomy than traditional public schools in exchange for increased accountability.[27] Individual charters and charter networks such as KIPP (Knowledge Is Power Program) develop charter schools in underserved communities, where the traditional public school system is especially inadequate, to prepare students for success in college and in life.[28] Charter schools not only aim to improve education for students. They also naturally help nearby public schools, which often suffer from overcrowding (thus overwhelmed public school teachers can perform better with a lowered student-teacher ratio) or administrative complacency (from lack of education market competition).

The Common Core program is a relatively new education standards program created to achieve better educational accountability and regain the United States' academic edge on the world stage. The joint state and federally supported program requires public schools across each state to follow its state-specific customized plan relating to the subjects of English and Math. This customized plan follows a standardized teaching agenda and testing schedule within each state. For a few reasons the program is a hotly contested topic in the political scene but not in a clear-cut partisan way. The Right typically takes more issue with Common Core than the Left, though both parties are internally divided.[29] Common Core is often

---

27   http://www.kipp.org/about-kipp/faq
28   http://www.kippnyc.org/about/kipp-national-network/
29   http://www.usnews.com/news/articles/2014/05/05/common-core-might-not-be-a-litmus-test-for-republican-candidates

criticized for, among other things, its "one-size-fits-all" model applied to an undeniably heterogeneous student population of diverse needs even within a given state. The Right is passionate in our belief that the local level can more appropriately address educational needs and goals of its children — some believe Common Core's statewide uniformity dismantles local level control. The Left is passionate in supporting teachers' unions, which protect teachers' rights and expectations from what they view as unreasonable work standards and responsibilities[30] — unions believe Common Core's testing requirement poses unreasonable work expectations. The debate continues, but with purely state-specific discretion and 46 states currently signed onto the program,[31] Common Core seems to at least be reasonable in its approach to state choice (consistent with conservative principles). The results coming from Common Core-states (e.g., student scores, teaching quality, actual learning) remain to be seen, but in time should indicate the program's efficacy.

One thing that both the Right and the Left can agree on: education reform is needed now more than ever. Among the international community, U.S. students' average test scores are underwhelming,[32] to put it mildly. The right kind of reform is important largely because U.S. students risk growing up unprepared to contribute to the prosperity of our society and to participate in the greater global economy. Our children's access to quality education in all communities, especially at-risk

---

30   http://www.nationalreview.com/article/371589/common-core-teachers-unions-think-again-frederick-m-hess

31   http://academicbenchmarks.com/common-core-state-adoption-map/

32   https://www.washingtonpost.com/local/education/us-students-lag-around-average-on-international-science-math-and-reading-test/2013/12/02/2e510f26-5b92-11e3-a49b-90a0e156254b_story.html

minority communities, directly impacts future successes, so we need a strong overall school system (i.e., public and alternative) to keep us competitive and therefore prosperous.

Affirmative Action

Liberal Accusation: You don't believe in providing minority students with admissions support considering the disadvantages they face.

BHC Counter: I do believe disadvantaged students of any background should be provided with support to compensate for the obstacles they experience and especially for those obstacles they overcame. My interpretation of "disadvantaged" is not focused on a specific skin tone, but rather on certain economic circumstances. Black and Hispanic students are statistically more likely to experience poverty, so a need-based affirmative action plan would remain supportive in assisting students of those backgrounds; but it would certainly not be predicated on skin color or ethnic background. In addition to low income, disadvantages come in various forms: health/ medical situations, family commitments (e.g., student worker), at-risk environment (e.g., neighborhood gangs), lack of parental guidance, and little access to reasonable education, to name a few. Given the various forms of disadvantages and the evident progress made toward racial equality, I support color-blind affirmative action policies recognizing any individual's strengths and personal story, which would cover handling disadvantaged circumstances.

Traditional race-based affirmative action was established in the 1960s in an effort to compensate for the results of the most shameful times in American history. Affirmative action programs often acted as a race-based "quota system."[33] At its inception and in years to follow, affirmative action facilitated efforts to integrate racially marginalized groups predominantly academically, as well as professionally, and subsequently socially and economically. The program was intended to be a means to an end — that is, the end of societally induced racial disadvantage. For example, periods of slavery, mandated racial segregation, and legal racial discrimination caused individual and generational disadvantages among black minorities.

Both Republican and Democratic politicians have recognized the nation's past failures to practice the American value of equality, and both have supported affirmative action laws in various forms for more than the past 50 years. Beyond legal policy, various types of institutions, such as universities and workplaces, have established their own affirmative action admissions and hiring practices. Because of *and* in tandem with these practices, discrimination has diminished and diversity has improved. Racism and other forms of civil discrimination are now not only legally prohibited but also culturally condemned in the mainstream of society.

At the risk of stating the obvious, the election of an African-American as the 44th president is a clear example of the progress made in the U.S. and the opportunities available to everyone regardless of skin color. Still, liberals claim race-based affirmative action remains necessary because they do not see *enough* progress. For instance, the popular vote results of the 2008 and 2012 elections troubled some liberals who were concerned that almost half of all voters did not support Obama, implying (and sometimes explicitly asserting) that

---

[33]   http://www.understandingrace.org/history/gov/begin_end_affirm.html

racial bias had an influential effect on many who did not vote for a black candidate.[34] However, these individuals should be pleasantly surprised to learn that in every presidential election won by a Democrat since 1940, the winner lost an average of 48% of the popular vote[35] — in line with Obama's results. There was no more or less bias against a black Democrat than there has been against white Democrats. Conservative voters (note, not racist voters or fanatical voters, but conservative voters) are committed to principles and not prejudice. We would readily vote for former Secretary of State Condoleezza Rice or Senator Tim Scott of South Carolina, for example, given their conservative values, over a person of any race with left-wing liberal politics centered on big government.

It is unclear when today's affirmative action supporters will have seen "enough progress" and subsequently agree to end the affirmative action era. Will "enough progress" be achieved when demographic surveys are equal across all racial, ethnic, and gender demographics? From the school campus to the office cubicle to the football field — this would be absolutely stifling to honest competition and meritocracy (not to mention mathematically impossible if taken literally). Alternatively, will "enough progress" be realized when all organizations reflect the nation's demographic composition, proportionately representing minority populations? This would imply participation rates of 13% black, 17% Hispanic, and 5% Asian,[36] and then each group to be split between men and women. For countless reasons, it is unreasonable to influence a given field to reflect the country's makeup. It would be excessively

---

34   http://www.newsbusters.org/blogs/noel-sheppard/2012/01/13/
      michael-moore-older-generations-didnt-vote-obama-are-racist
35   http://uselectionatlas.org/RESULTS/
36   http://quickfacts.census.gov/qfd/states/00000.html

calculating (and extremely unmeritocratic) to try to artificially generate (that is "force") those numbers.

Additionally, we see today's excessive affirmative action policies producing unintended consequences, many at odds with the intended benefits. Dinesh D'Souza of *The Dartmouth Review* sees *today's* affirmative action strengthening a "suspicion that [blacks] might be intellectually inferior."[37] Attorney General Loretta Lynch, a Democrat and an African-American woman, believes that traditional affirmative action "has come to have a great deal of baggage attached to it."[38] When well-qualified black minorities are *assumed* to have benefitted from affirmative action policies, rather than having earned their positions on a level playing field, the prevailing institution of race-based affirmative action unfavorably serves those minorities.

Affirmative action has been defined as "positive discrimination."[39] The dictionary also defines discrimination as "the unjust or prejudicial treatment of different categories of people or things, especially on the grounds of race, age, or sex."[40] We realize that "positive" discrimination is effectively problematic. As with physics, where every action has an equal and opposite reaction, *positive* discrimination towards one person is countered by *negative* discrimination against another. As a result, more unintended consequences of affirmative action come at the

---

[37] http://www.amazon.com/Letters-Young-Conservative-Art-Mentoring/dp/0465017347

[38] http://www.nytimes.com/2015/01/13/us/politics/loretta-lynch-attorney-general-nominee.html?_r=0

[39] http://www.oxforddictionaries.com/us/definition/american_english/affirmative-action

[40] http://www.oxforddictionaries.com/us/definition/american_english/discrimination

expense of politically unrecognized minority categories or the merely deserving but visually "generic" individual (yes, many, through no fault of their own, may be a variety of white). Sadly, the problem society was looking to deservedly rectify has warped: where we were once fighting for antidiscrimination laws in the name of equality and diversity, now a liberal portion of our society is fighting for discriminatory antidiscrimination laws (got that?). We now have socially acceptable discriminatory practices, for example, in which Asians may need to score as much as 450 SAT points higher than that of other demographics to be admitted into the same university program.[41]

With the remarkable progress that has been made through antidiscrimination legal protections and diversity awareness initiatives, Americans of every race, ethnicity, and gender have demonstrated that a level of success can be achieved corresponding to the level of effort exerted. Given the evidence of these realities, society ought to evolve from a debilitating dependence on race-based affirmative action programs. We want to see all Americans achieve through individual self-empowerment, rooted in principles of equal rights and opportunities. And where Americans may lack opportunities given financial circumstance, a socioeconomic-based affirmative action plan should serve to help equalize this type of inequality. Dr. Martin Luther King Jr. envisioned an affirmative action plan like this, one which all Americans, truly blind to skin color, could support: "I do not intend that this program of economic aid apply only to the Negro; it should benefit the disadvantaged of all races."[42]

---

[41]   http://www.economist.com/news/briefing/21669595-asian-americans-are-united-states-most-successful-minority-they-are-complaining-ever

[42]   http://www.alex-haley.com/alex_haley_martin_luther_king_interview.htm

Pledge of Allegiance

Liberal Accusation: You believe it's okay to force students to recite the Pledge of Allegiance to the American flag.

BHC Counter: I believe it is symbolically and culturally important to *encourage* children to participate in the national tradition of reciting the Pledge of Allegiance at the start of the school day, particularly the public school day. It would be unconstitutional to force anyone to recite the Pledge, but I see nothing wrong with facilitating public displays of patriotism. Many Americans have dedicated and sacrificed their lives for this country to become a beacon of freedom, prosperity, good will, and realized dreams — realities we enjoy today and ideals we continually strive for. The flag serves as a symbol of our nation and its ideals; reciting the Pledge to the American flag demonstrates a brief yet respectful appreciation for these. I view this as basic patriotism, regardless of your political or apolitical stripes.

Public schools are a common place for the Pledge to be recited but unfortunately a place where the Pledge is sometimes contested. We believe that at institutions of public education, where students and teachers benefit from American taxpayers' support, a gesture of national respect is reasonable. Nevertheless, it is shocking how many times this seemingly innocuous practice has seen its day in court, all the way up to the U.S. Supreme Court.[43] Those who oppose the Pledge may cite constitutional objections; however, public schools are rife with restrictions of otherwise expected freedoms (e.g., dress

---

[43] https://www.washingtonpost.com/news/volokh-conspiracy/wp/2014/05/09/under-god-in-pledge-of-allegiance-is-constitutional-says-massachusettss-highest-court/

code, inappropriate language, cell phone use) in order to instill respect in our children.

Some on the Left feel public school or government time allotted to our national Pledge is potentially offensive and encroaches on a constitutional right to free speech, as well as separation of church and state. The Pledge often includes the mention of "God," which some nonbelievers find offensive. Perhaps to their surprise, reciting the Pledge does not demand or request a belief in this God, or any supreme being. In fact, the "under God" portion of the Pledge can be skipped if one feels so compelled. The Pledge simply offers its citizens an opportunity to acknowledge our great country, founded under Judeo-Christian influence (hence the spiritual shout-out), of *liberty and justice for all*. We believe that Americans should stand proudly and voice the Pledge with sincerity, keeping in mind the values which are represented by the flag. We recognize that some people are uncomfortable making that pledge, but we hope that they too will recognize, in their own way, that our country is worth honoring.

> I pledge allegiance to the Flag of the United States of America, and to the Republic for which it stands, one Nation under God, indivisible, with liberty and justice for all.[44]

Rights

Conservatives take the acts of defining and defending Americans' rights, particularly the *equality* of those rights, very

---

44   http://www.senate.gov/reference/resources/pdf/RL30243.pdf

seriously. Rights serve as a shield against big government overreach. Our belief in rights extends to our appreciation for the nuances among kinds of rights — inalienable rights vs. civil rights vs. state's rights vs. religious rights vs. human rights — and how they play into our nation's Constitution. In spite of various classifications of rights, we unequivocally understand that they should apply to every American equally. Nevertheless, liberals regularly accuse conservatives of denying rights to certain Americans based on prejudices against certain sexual orientations, races, socioeconomic situations, and so on. This accusation would be cause for serious concern if it were true, but it is not. Unfortunately, healthy exchange becomes difficult given that many liberals express their opposition to conservative views by mischaracterizing our beliefs and distorting our objectives. They apply this deceptive practice especially to the politics of rights issues. Whether they honestly misunderstand our position, or they intentionally mischaracterize it, is tough to determine. However, a productive debate cannot occur if the opposing side is unable or unwilling to truly understand (not necessarily agree with, but simply hear out) diversity of opinion.

Marriage Equality

Liberal Accusation: You do not believe in same-sex marriage.

BHC Counter: Actually, I think that any consenting, committed and loving adult couple should be allowed to marry and that the gender(s) of a couple should be irrelevant as it relates to civil marriage. A properly limited government should not involve itself in this matter. I view principles such as equality for all and separation of church and state as supporting legislation in favor of marriage for gay and lesbian couples. Although not invalid to generalize Republicans as supportive of the traditional religious definition of marriage, categorizing all conservatives as against same-sex marriages is simply false — just ask LGBT Republicans and Log Cabin Republican supporters.[45]

Our support for same-sex marriage is not only related to "technicalities" of separation of church and state and limited government. Conservatives generally believe that a married couple is the responsible foundation of raising a cohesive family, and in turn the institution of family is a building block of prosperous society. So from a practical standpoint, we believe two adults of any gender combination who embrace responsibility, commitment, and love can be equally equipped to contribute to our country's prosperous future built on marriage, family, and community.

To address an assertion of those who strongly favor traditional marriage, it has been suggested that children raised by heterosexual parents are better developed than children raised by homosexual parents. While we do not believe this to be the case, more objectively speaking, conclusive evidence to validate this claim is lacking. It is not possible for a legitimate study to have been conducted given a lack of significant data among non-marginalized married homosexual parents. The simple fact is that gay adoption and gay marriage were not common or even legal until recently, thereby making it unlikely that relevant, comparable data points could have been studied.

While we are of the opinion that marriage should apply to same-sex couples, we also believe in the freedom of religion and therefore respect a considerable portion of our population's

---

[45]   http://www.logcabin.org/

opinion that religious marriage is between one man and one woman (nearly 40% of Republicans as *well as* Democrats favor traditional marriage).[46] To claim that this belief is ignorant or wrong is an intolerant way to defend tolerance. Thankfully, there are members on both sides who can agree that religion should have no bearing on the issue of marriage equality. The Gay & Lesbian Advocates & Defenders (GLAD) organization writes, "The discussion is about ending governmental discrimination against gay and lesbian families with respect to civil marriage and its legal protections and responsibilities — not about any religious rite of marriage. Every faith is and will remain free to set its own rules about who can marry and on what terms."[47] Unfortunately however, reality has shown recent situations in which government overreach sided against an individual's religious freedom; for example religious photographers and bakers wishing to abstain from working for gay marriage ceremonies have resulted in hefty court-ordered fines and forced service obligations.[48] We find this unreasonable, similar to how we once found government overreach in barring a same-sex couple's wish to be married.

At the core of the same-sex marriage debate is the fact that definitions and laws surrounding *civil* marriage were borrowed largely from religious traditions regarding marriage. Civil marriage was structured this way because it reflected the

---

[46] http://www.people-press.org/2015/06/08/same-sex-marriage-detailed-tables/?utm_expid=53098246-2.Lly4CFSVQG2lphsg-Koplg.0&utm_referrer=http%3A%2F%2Fwww.people-press.org%2F2015%2F07%2F29%2Fnegative-views-of-supreme-court-at-record-high-driven-by-republican-dissatisfaction%2F

[47] https://www.glad.org/uploads/docs/publications/cu-vs-marriage.pdf

[48] http://www.npr.org/2013/12/10/250098572/no-cake-for-you-saying-i-dont-to-same-sex-marriage%20

collective view of the American public during a vastly different time in our country's history — at its inception. We doubt that a sinister intention of discriminating against openly gay couples in the future factored into the wording of laws. But times change and so do our perspectives on certain key issues. What was considered by the majority of our citizens as normal then could be considered discriminatory now. However, it is important to acknowledge that legal discrimination is not unique to the issue of same-sex marriage. We as a country observe laws that may restrict the rights of a cross section of our citizens because of the shared opinion of a majority legislated by elected representation or because of our Constitution. For example, a 20-year-old American, an adult who may serve and die for his country, is legally restricted from buying a beer; or the patriotic, qualified, but naturalized American citizen who wishes to run for president is legally prohibited from holding such office. More relevant restrictions involving marriage rights prohibit two consenting adults from marrying because they happen to be of close familial relations. These are not necessarily acts of discrimination, but rather legal judgments made when the matters were addressed.

It had been clear to us for some time that the matter of same-sex marriage needed to be addressed. Like so many societal matters involving popular opinion and norms changing faster than legal documents and government bureaucracy, we first refer to our Constitution. Our Founders drafted the Constitution in part to guide us through addressing what they expected to be inevitably changing times and circumstance. While we firmly believe, per the Constitution, that laws are most representative when made at state and local levels, we recognize scenarios in which a state-by-state solution is unreasonable (e.g., national defense) and when the federal government must provide consistent legal guidance across state lines. Same-sex marriage is one of those cases given the state-to-state portability of married couples and the practical significance of universal recognition of spousal rights. Therefore, marriage laws are an issue which needs federal legislative attention, as a state-specific determination merely acts as a Band-Aid providing piecemeal solutions.

In the summer of 2015, the U.S. Supreme Court took on the landmark same-sex marriage case of Obergefell v. Hodges, and ruled 5-4 in favor of same-sex marriage.[49] While we agree with the majority opinion, we disagree with the notion that a matter of this nature may be decided upon by a majority (in this case by a margin of *one*) of nine *unelected* Supreme Court judges; the right to marry is not a civil right nor is it a constitutional matter (in other words, it is not mentioned in the Constitution), so we do not see the judicial prudence behind defining an activity outside the jurisdiction of the Supreme Court. Four Supreme Court judges held the same opinion. Many may feel that the ends justify the means, nevertheless it does not take away from the fact that this very significant issue was passed in a very gray manner. As Justice Roberts suggested in his dissenting opinion, "Stealing this issue from the people will for many cast a cloud over same-sex marriage, making a dramatic social change that much more difficult to accept." Justice Scalia's dissenting opinion elaborates, "Today's decree says that my Ruler, and the Ruler of 320 million Americans coast-to-coast, is a majority of the nine lawyers on the Supreme Court."[50]

---

[49]   http://www.scotusblog.com/case-files/cases/obergefell-v-hodges/

[50]   http://www.usnews.com/news/articles/2015/06/26/9-need-to-know-quotes-from-the-obergefell-v-hodges-opinions

To Justice Scalia's point, we would support a same-sex marriage bill sent to Congress for our elected officials to vote based on the strength of public opinion. If a bill is defeated due to lack of national consensus, state-by-state rulings must be accepted as an imperfect piecemeal solution until a unified solution coalesces, or until the collective voice strengthens for reform. Support of same-sex marriage is a personal belief to which everyone is entitled; however, it is not the personal belief, but rather the *collective* personal belief which makes law in a democratic republic (i.e., the U.S.). We are of the opinion that the strength of today's collective American majority belief in favor of same-sex marriage[51] can be expressed by appropriate, lawful procedure.

Voting Rights

Liberal Accusation: Your support for voter ID laws is a proxy for racial and low-income voter discrimination.

BHC Counter: I unequivocally believe that every American citizen over 18 years old, regardless of race or socioeconomic status, has the right to vote in public elections. I believe that the constitutional right to vote is a uniquely significant right, because it exemplifies a democracy — one person, one vote. That vote should be protected so that its integrity is never compromised or put at risk. Otherwise, voter fraud, which can occur by people inclined toward any party, has the potential for statewide and nationwide repercussions. Voter fraud is a form of identity theft and can happen when a person votes under the guise of another person's voter registration. To

---

51   http://www.pewforum.org/2015/07/29/graphics-slideshow-changing-attitudes-on-gay-marriage/

prevent this, I support efforts such as the photo identification requirement to verify that a voter is who he or she claims to be. I think it safe to assume that identity theft has bipartisan opposition; nevertheless, photo ID law aiming to prevent voter fraud has become a very divisive politicized debate. The truth is conservatives simply want to keep our democratic system accountable, no different from our emphasis on accountability in all areas (e.g., gun-related background checks; see Gun Control section).

The recent heated debate regarding the requirement, or lack thereof, to show a government-issued photo ID at the voting booth has become a gravely distorted issue. Liberals believe that requiring a government-issued ID upon voting only serves to discriminate against minorities and poor Americans (i.e., largely Democrat-voter demographics[52]), because they are less likely to have a state or federal photo ID. To the contrary, we believe minorities and low-income Americans are capable (it is prejudice to deem them *incapable*) of applying for a government-issued ID, especially given that they would have already proven themselves capable of applying for voter registration. The qualification requiring that a citizen must first register in order to vote demonstrates that the constitutional right to vote is not unconditional — an idea similar to how we (and liberals much more so) view the constitutional, yet conditional (e.g., upon thorough background checks) right to bear arms. But beyond this, nearly every American citizen either files a tax return or applies for government assistance in one or many forms (e.g., welfare, Medicaid). These actions require administrative efforts on the part of the citizen, including showing government-issued

---

52   https://www.washingtonpost.com/news/the-fix/wp/2015/04/08/the-10-most-loyal-demographic-groups-for-republicans-and-democrats/

photo ID. So as we see it, the task of getting a photo ID for voter accountability is far from logistically unreasonable.

A government-issued photo ID is required for activities encompassing the entire socioeconomic spectrum: applying for food stamps or Social Security, purchasing alcohol and cigarettes, buying an R-rated movie ticket, driving a car, and passing through airport security. This allows a person to verify that he or she is who he or she claims to be and is legally permitted to receive the benefit, good, or service. We believe that an act as important and nationally influential as voting should also require official photo identification. Proof of identification simply aims to maintain the integrity of democracy, our nation's elected offices, and individual rights (individuals of *all* races and income classes). For the sake of compromise and efficiency, rather than argue over the practicality of having a government-issued photo ID, we would back a solution whereby issued voter registration cards include the citizen's photograph.

Civil Rights

Liberal Accusation: You do not care about the civil rights of minority groups.

BHC Counter: I believe that all Americans, by virtue of being U.S. citizens and regardless of minority or majority group classification, are guaranteed basic civil rights. Civil rights are those freedoms and protections specifically outlined in the Constitution as well as by congressional legislation, and are intended to apply to everyone equally. I would find any practice demonstrating civil rights violations as unacceptable and requiring redress. While I believe the history of our nation is remarkable, it is not without shameful blunders with regard to upholding civil rights. We are proud of the fact that our nation regrets, corrects, and learns from such grave civil missteps.

Both Republicans and Democrats have led the way in civil rights movements. These efforts have shaped our nation, most famously beginning with our first Republican president, Abraham Lincoln, and his passionate opposition to slavery. In 1863 he issued the Emancipation Proclamation declaring, "All persons held as slaves... are, and henceforward shall be free."[53] Following the abolishment of slavery during the Reconstruction Era of the South, southern Republicans, including whites and newly freed blacks, were subjected to violent attacks by white supremacist groups like the Ku Klux Klan, which were dominated by white Democrats resentful of their loss of power.[54] However, we understand that radical extremists can infiltrate any party, religion, or organization, so it is inaccurate and morally wrong to use them to slanderously generalize the entire population of a group (e.g., negative generalizations and slanderous criticisms against conservatives or liberals).

Civil rights advocates made major advancements over the next hundred years. The Fifteenth Amendment, which gave the vote to all American men regardless of race, was passed by a majority Republican Congress in 1870.[55] Later, the then decades-old Women's Suffrage movement culminated in 1920

---

53 http://www.archives.gov/exhibits/featured_documents/emancipation_proclamation/transcript.html
54 http://www.pbs.org/wgbh/americanexperience/features/general-article/grant-kkk/
55 http://www.history.com/this-day-in-history/15th-amendment-adopted

with the Nineteenth Amendment recognizing women's right to vote.[56] This movement was pioneered by Republican women, most famously Susan B. Anthony, and the Amendment was first introduced in Congress by Republican Senator Aaron Sargent. The Suffragists' unofficial headquarters, The Women's National Republican Club, founded by Suffragette leader Henrietta Wells Livermore in 1921, still stands in midtown Manhattan and continues to operate as a center for conservative-minded political discussion.

A more recent era of American civil rights movements secured legal recognition and federal protection of citizenship for black Americans in the 1960s. While this was a predominantly Democratic Party-led initiative, just like in past civil rights advancements, this was not the result of single-party partisan support. Dr. Martin Luther King Jr. famously and peacefully led this movement; his political stance was clear: "Someone must remain in the position of non-alignment, so that he can look objectively at both parties and be the conscience of both."[57] Civil rights should not be viewed as a Democrat versus Republican issue, because throughout history and in the present day, both political parties have played instrumental roles in protecting various categories of civil rights, such as race, religion, and gender. Civil rights should be viewed as a bipartisan American issue. We understand Dr. King's belief in the need to look objectively within a given party. To the Republican Party's credit (and sometimes disservice), many members do make objective judgments rather than blindly running with the party's platform. This results in internal party debates (e.g., Tea Party

---

[56]   http://www.usconstitutionday.us/p/19th-amendment.html
[57]   http://www.all-famous-quotes.com/Martin_Luther_King_Jr_quotes.
         html

versus Establishment) for which the GOP has at times been undeservingly criticized.

Our core principle of equality for all intrinsically supports our recognition of equitably upheld civil rights. Civil rights in the context of constitutional rights (to which it is often but not necessarily referred) involve those freedoms specifically outlined in the Constitution (e.g., religion, speech, assembly, bear arms, vote). Our appreciation for a precise understanding of the intention and design of our Constitution is often the crux of our diverging approaches to political thought and legal questions. A conservative's emphasis on literal accuracy guides us on how we read and then abide by or modify rights and laws. This contrasts to a liberal's emphasis on interpretation which guides them to read and subjectively interpret rights and laws. We believe that a liberal interpretation has the tendency to overstep into areas outside constitutional jurisdiction and into the realm reserved for a legislative body to decide. For example, marriage equality has been pop-politicized as the present-day civil rights issue. While our beliefs in support of same-sex marriage differ from our Party's current stance on the issue, we understand marriage equality is *not* a constitutional rights matter (see Marriage Equality section). For this reason, conservatives believe the issue ought to be reserved not for the judicial branch, but rather for state government or, ideally, federal congressional legislation (e.g., the civil rights acts of the 1960s).

Throughout U.S. history the beneficiaries of civil rights have been as diverse as the proponents of its movements — that absolutely includes Republicans. Unfortunately, our Party's support for civil rights has been snubbed and current political debates have been denigrated by the Left into emotionally divisive pits. The liberal claim that conservatives look to deny anyone of his or her civil rights is absurd and insulting. We stand firmly by the promise of civil rights equality for each and every American given our respect for the law and our basic moral compass.

Euthanasia

Liberal Accusation: You want to deny an individual's personal decision to his or her own right to life.

BHC Counter: I believe that the grave unintended consequences which come with legalized euthanasia or assisted suicide policy must be avoided. Arriving at an opinion on this issue is certainly a struggle, especially given my belief in an individual's free will and recognition that medical circumstances could be so dire that one would consider terminating his or her own life. I sincerely sympathize with someone who, for example, is terminally suffering and lacks the will to continue living. At the same time, my regard for all human life, from the womb to hospice, makes me think that willfully ending an innocent life is not a solution — there ought to be a better alternative to euthanasia.

Rather than relying entirely on a rudimentary belief in free will, we must consider the devastating unintended consequences (e.g., conflicts of interest) which would arise and compromise even the best-intentioned euthanasia policy. A person's life is one's most fundamental possession, and we should critically examine any situation, including self-selecting, in which a person can be deprived of that. For example, where a person in extreme medical distress might choose euthanasia, free will and sound mind could very well be in an unstable state. In this scenario it is impossible to determine what might have been decided at a time when that person was of sound mind.

Under legalized euthanasia or assisted suicide, the family and doctor of a patient could very likely play an influential role in the life-or-death decision of that patient. In an environment where definitions and diagnoses are subject to revisions and interpretations, who is to define and decide critical factors such as "terminal" or "sound mind"? Even if laws attempted to avoid vague situations left up to subjective interpretation, the matter is vulnerable to perversities of intent and interpretation. Health care costs, the burden of a dependent elder, and the temptation of inheritance from a relative are all pressures which might be inappropriately considered when making a decision under legalized euthanasia.

Unfortunately, the reality is that vulnerable people cannot be fully protected (nor can they always be definitively identified as vulnerable) from exploitation under legal euthanasia or assisted suicide policies. As for situations involving a sound-minded terminally suffering individual, we would advocate for experts and legislators to offer effective and reasonable options (e.g., pain management, quality hospice care, psychological or psychiatric therapy) in place of allowing someone to kill himself or herself. We understand that there is no simple solution to this very complicated and unfortunate scenario; however, we want to help people prevent suffering and maintain dignity — and hopefully avoid the likeliest fate by finding a way to recover. Until there is a perfect solution, one in which a law allows the free will of a sound mind to be exercised without the serious risks of unintended consequences, we find it irresponsible to the individual and society to legalize euthanasia or assisted suicide.

Women's Issues

Conservatives view *all* fiscal, social, and foreign policy issues — jobs, education, taxes, security, health care, and so on — as relevant to women. In other words, all political issues are women's issues. We understand, though, that most liberal activists and the media have reduced "women's issues" to primarily be shorthand for sexual and reproductive matters. With this connotation (an arguably sexist one, at that) and given our perspective on these matters, liberals accuse conservatives of waging a "war on women." Alarming alliteration is quite catchy, but that doesn't make the accusation true. As a woman, I am intimately familiar with what is pop-politically meant by "women's issues," and as a conservative woman I am confident that conservatives or Republicans (48% of whom are women[58]) are not waging a war against women. I have noticed this liberal attack strategy with predictable frequency — a shocking catchphrase is publicized to provoke feelings (not necessarily realities) of injustice and victimization. The goal of the liberal-generated "conservative war on women" movement is to scare female voters away from supporting Republicans. But contrary to claims by the Left, the fundamental issues we stand for are actually blind to gender, as well as race, ethnicity, and other labels. Conservatives categorically believe women are equal to men and men are equal to women.

Abortion

Liberal Accusation: You do not believe a woman has the right to choose.

---

[58]   http://www.people-press.org/2012/08/23/a-closer-look-at-the-parties-in-2012/

BHC Counter: I believe that all Americans — female and male — have rights and more importantly *equal* rights to live and act as they see appropriate within legal boundaries. All innocent human beings are inherently worthy of these rights, and if they are fortunate enough to be in the U.S., then these rights are legally protected. Given this belief, the decision to abort is, in a sense, an act of age-based exploitation — unlike a pregnant woman, a baby living within a pregnant woman is without a voice and a vote in the matter (quite literally its own matter). But perhaps I digress. To literally answer the infamously controversial question, I unequivocally believe that a woman, just like a man, has the right to choose... an education, career, life choices, but not necessarily to choose the death of a human being in a womb. With regard purely to policy implementation, I believe abortion should not be used as a form of birth control; however, circumstances such as health threats, rape, incest, and (more controversially) *very* early-term decision warrant concessions.

Irrelevant to religious teachings and very relevant to biology, we understand that the moment of conception triggers the start of human life. At that point, conservatives believe the unborn baby has its own right to life; this makes a mother's decision to abort become the alternative (to put it mildly) to that baby's life. In paraphrasing an old American adage "your rights end where another's begin,"[59] the pro-life argument begins. It is shameful that the pro-abortion argument is exploited through a simple, nebulously-worded, faux civil rights chant about a "woman's right to choose." "Reproductive rights" is another liberal alliterative mantra embraced by abortion supporters. If this debate were in fact literally about reproductive rights,

---

[59]   http://quoteinvestigator.com/category/zechariah-chafee/

then we would be in agreement. We wholeheartedly agree that everyone has the right to reproduce human life — and contraceptives can help avoid unintentionally exercising that right (see Contraception section). Separately, we do not agree that everyone has the right to destroy human life (i.e., abort human life). The Right–Left ideological disconnect involves the meaning of reproduction: we believe reproduction implies pregnancy, while they believe reproduction implies birth. Since we acknowledge existence of human life upon impregnation, reproductive rights are technically (i.e., biologically) exercised at the point of conceiving. Finding the loophole in this "technicality" is how pro-abortion activists misrepresent abortion to become yet another "right" that awful Republicans try to take away.

The pro-abortion position (more popularly known as "pro-choice," considering that the word "abortion" sounds quite unpleasant and the actual procedure of aborting is even more so) is one which draws on justifications involving the pregnant woman's free will, the "good" of the unborn/unwanted child, and the benefits to greater society. The first argument in support of the pregnant woman's free will (which we believe entirely rejects the unborn baby's free will in favor of the mother's free will) is largely ideological, but really nothing new in the abortion debate. However, the latter two arguments — the "good" of the unborn/unwanted child and the benefits to greater society — are some which have many pro-choicers espousing "data-backed" support for a pro-choice culture. The theory, which is popularly referenced in the pop-economic book *Freakonomics,* points to a correlation between reduced crime rates in the late 20th century following the 1973 ruling of Roe v. Wade.[60] This has

---

60   Freakonomics, Steven Levitt and Stephen Dubner, Chapter 4, ISBN 0-06-123400-1, April 2005

eased many pro-choicers' consciences given the underlying idea that unwanted children or children born to parents who cannot support them are more likely to live crime-ridden or ill-fated lives. First, correlation does not imply causation; but that is just a technicality compared to our central opposition to this argument. *Freakonomics* makes a case that children who would have otherwise been born into poverty and in turn participate in criminal activity were salvaged from such a life — because they were aborted before they could be born. So operating under this "logic," perhaps the children were not around to allegedly contribute to society's crime rates; but this immoral and otherwise flawed logic also implies that abortion is reasonable, even beneficial, if the child is expected to be born into poor conditions (speaking of discriminatory socioeconomic profiling). This specific type of self-righteous, disturbing rationalization draws parallels to the crooked rationalization once made for slaveholding practices. (Note: this observation is absolutely *not* equating a pro-choice stance to slaveholding, but rather comparing a specific disconcerting thought process cited in the abortion debate.) Slave owners viewed themselves as benevolent masters of black slaves who were inferior in nature. They defended slavery practices with arguments ranging from economic (i.e., the greater society) to humanitarian (i.e., the "good" of an uncivilized and helpless species).[61] The reality, of course, is that in spite of all the justification or reasoning, the "well-intentioned" conviction of one individual's choice simply cannot be imposed on another individual, particularly when livelihood is at stake.

Contrary to the liberal depiction of conservatives as pro-life religious zealots espousing inferiority of women and their

---

[61]   http://www.ushistory.org/us/27f.asp

rights, we would point you to President Reagan's view. He said, "With me, abortion is not a problem of religion, it's a problem of the Constitution. I believe that until and unless someone can establish that the unborn child is not a living human being, then that child is already protected by the Constitution, which guarantees, life, liberty, and the pursuit of happiness to all of us."[62] The focus of our perspective is on the life (planned or unplanned) versus the planned death of an unborn baby. While some pro-choice advocates take solace in their position by referring to a baby in utero as an embryo or fetus, using these scientific terms does not make the reality of what takes place, that is, the termination of a human life, any different.

That said, many conservatives, including mainstream and elected officials (especially members of The Wish List, a pro-choice Republican organization), understand that it is inappropriate to hold an exclusively pro-life stance. Many of us are in agreement with limiting the decision to abort within the earlier stages of a pregnancy. While we stand by the belief that abortion should not be used as a form of birth control to terminate unwanted pregnancies, we know that a strictly pro-life law could at times result in extremely tragic life circumstances. With competing factors at stake, balancing the rights of the unborn child with those of the mother steers us to a compromise. The will of the mother is a concern which may certainly act as an overriding factor. We support concessions for abortion under severe health threats to the mother or the child, and in cases of rape or incest. We do not believe that life is any less worthy when conceived under such dreadful conditions, which is why these exceptions are called out as *concessions*. So while we agree to these

---

[62]   http://www.reaganfoundation.org/reagan-quotes-detail.
aspx?tx=2041

concessions, we acknowledge that the decision remains morally distressing.

Access to abortion today is legislated by each state, with 41 states imposing a given time-sensitive limit on abortion (nine states and D.C. allow abortions even through the ninth month of pregnancy).[63] Many conservatives are agreeable to a first-trimester abortion limitation (i.e., about 14 weeks into pregnancy), though only two states observe a term limit like this. Some states observe a 20- to 22-week limit; this timing is based largely on the reality that doctors routinely perform life-saving surgeries on unborn babies at 20 weeks or older. For instance, these surgeries involve giving anesthesia to the fetus in order to numb his or her pain caused by surgical incisions. So if we act to protect 20-week term babies from pain, then logic and compassion lead us to believe we should look to protect them from death. Most states observe an abortion ban after the second trimester (i.e., about 28 weeks into pregnancy), at which point a fetus is deemed viable outside the womb. That unfortunately still leaves nine states and D.C. with no specific time limits or restrictions on abortion. A pregnant woman could abort her unborn baby a day before his or her birth day. We find this to be reprehensible.

The pro-choice/pro-life debate will inevitably continue, as it is an issue deeply enveloped by emotion on both sides. What should *absolutely not* continue are slanderous accusations of our "war on women" and denial of "reproductive rights," as well as general liberal cynicism around our compassion for all innocent human life. We are not taking rights away from

---

[63]   http://www.nytimes.com/interactive/2013/06/18/us/politics/abortion-restrictions.html?_r=1&

women; rather, we are acknowledging the rights of a human life living within his or her mother's womb. Our compassion and respect for the right to life should not be demonized into something other than what it is: equal consideration of the life of a voiceless unborn baby.

Contraception

Liberal Accusation: You oppose women's access to and use of contraception.

BHC Counter: I strongly support access to all safe methods of contraception such as condoms, birth control pills, and intrauterine devices (known as IUDs). I absolutely view contraception as highly preferable to abortion with regard to handling unwanted pregnancies. Techniques which responsibly *prevent* pregnancy have everything to do with the conservative principle of self-responsibility. I also support contraceptives for its integral role in workplace gender equality by giving women greater flexibility to control and/or time decisions between career and motherhood.

The completely false impression that we reject the use of contraceptives originates from misleading liberal propaganda. First, unlike what some liberals espouse, extremely religious conservatives who may oppose contraception compose an extreme subset which is not representative of mainstream conservatism (see Applicable Extremism section). Second, the actual political debate centers on the means by which a person's contraception is funded. The controversy emerges in two scenarios, both involving government intervention: government using public taxpayer money to cover the costs of an individual's contraception purchases, and government forcing private religious organizations and business owners to offer employee insurance plans which cover specific controversial forms of birth control. This includes post-intercourse birth controls/abortifacient agents, like the "morning-after pill," which often takes effect by inducing a miscarriage (a deliberate miscarriage is an abortion). We see the latter as an infringement on religious freedom.

Under the Affordable Care Act (ACA; also known as Obamacare), birth control pills are fully covered by publically-subsidized health insurance plans. We view the allocation of public taxpayer dollars toward non-medical elective contraception as inappropriate and fiscally inefficient (see Health Care section). Birth control is typically not a "health"-related matter, as health is the state of being free from illness or injury.[64] Barring rare unfortunate circumstances, becoming pregnant is not an illness or an injury. Juxtapose this to antibiotics, vaccinations, and MRIs, for example, which *are* health-related measures. Furthermore, while disease, hunger, poverty, and an inadequate education system are just a few problematic realities in need of public support, we view government-sponsored contraception as pickpocketing from public funding priorities.

We recognize that elements of this debate warrant honest discussion — not one-sided liberal declarations boiled down to the tediously misused chant for "reproductive rights" (see Abortion section). If this were really about reproductive rights, then government-subsidized Viagra should also be a demanded entitlement. The debate should actually focus around two suboptimal realities: taxpayer money funding the recreational

---

64   http://www.oxforddictionaries.com/us/definition/american_english/
     health

sexual intercourse of others (taking from priority areas in need of funding) versus accidental pregnancies putting financial and emotional strain on an unprepared single mother and her child, requiring greater and longer-term taxpayer support.

Ultimately, we support the use of contraception and we can understand that some degree of public subsidy for it (e.g., means-tested Medicaid) might have to be a near-term small cost in exchange for a longer-term large benefit. However, we are against government forcing religious groups or employers to provide free contraceptives, particularly controversial abortifacient agents such as the "morning-after pill." And more broadly we oppose the ACA's full coverage mandate which has taxpayers essentially supporting another person's recreational sexual activity, or more controversially, a deliberate miscarriage. To be sexually active without "consequence" is a very personal preference but it is certainly not a right, especially not one that ends up as the financial responsibility of others.

Equal Pay

Liberal Accusation: You do not support a woman's right to receive equal pay for equal work.

BHC Counter: I absolutely believe that all women and men should receive equal pay for equal work. Not only do I believe it, but I am certain that current Equal Pay Act legislation, originally introduced by Republican Congresswoman Winifred Stanley in 1942,[65] makes this practice of equality the law. As a conservative I believe that our meritocratic society means we

---

[65] http://www.politico.com/story/2009/06/equal-pay-bill-introduced-june-19-1944-023892

should respect and adhere to the principle of equality for all and favoritism to none.

Unfortunately, this principle has not always been observed. It is widely acknowledged that American women have suffered a long history of gender-based discrimination and subordination. Inspirational movements such as women's suffrage, spearheaded by female Republicans, have helped make great strides towards gender equality. Today we find ourselves in a society which recognizes and continues to encourage improvements in gender equality; though conservatives and liberals have varied perspectives on the degree of progress our nation has made here and ideas on how to approach continued improvements in this realm.

"Equal pay for equal work" is the call chanted by the Left after a Census Bureau statistic revealed that on average, a woman earns $0.77 for every $1.00 a man earns.[66] Before becoming alarmed by assumed injustice, we want to understand the story which drives these numbers. Liberals looking to make a gender inequality claim are either unaware or fail to mention that this Census Bureau statistic averages the incomes of *all* female earners, many of whom choose to work in lower-paying but more personally rewarding professions (e.g., teaching or nursing). Also included in this statistic are women who are part-time employees (working mothers) or have fewer years of workforce experience (younger or returning after time off for motherhood). The Bureau compares this to the average income of *all* male earners, many of whom make career choices different from those of females — the generalized "equal

---

66   http://www.washingtonexaminer.com/no-women-do-not-make-77-cents-for-every-dollar-men-make/article/2546931

work" portion of the protest is really not so equal after all. Male earners typically opt for higher-paying but higher stress professions, a variable which happens to correlate with why men die earlier than women. (Where are the protests against gender life span inequality?)

Other non-discriminatory variables which influence pay occur before women begin their careers. As one NPR correspondent noted, "Women are overrepresented among majors that don't pay very well (psychology, art, comparative literature), and underrepresented in lots of lucrative majors (most fields in engineering)."[67] A writer from *The Daily Beast* (who also happens to be a woman) expands on the point:

> Much of the wage gap can be explained away by simply taking account of college majors. Early childhood educators and social workers can expect to earn around $36,000 and $39,000, respectively. By contrast, petroleum engineering and metallurgy degrees promise median earnings of $120,000 and $80,000. Not many aspiring early childhood educators would change course once they learn they can earn more in metallurgy or mining... Women, far more than men, appear to be drawn to jobs in the caring professions; and men are more likely to turn up in people-free zones. In the pursuit of happiness, men and women appear to take different paths... If a woman wants to be a teacher rather than a miner... more power to her.[68]

---

67   http://www.npr.org/sections/money/2013/09/11/220748057/why-women-like-me-choose-lower-paying-jobs

68   http://www.thedailybeast.com/articles/2014/02/01/no-women-don-t-make-less-money-than-men.html

The college major component, blind to gender, contributes to a lower average salary for women versus men. With that settled at least in our minds, we remain interested in the results after isolating for these variables. When analyzing apples-to-apples (i.e., men and women of the same profession, tenure, educational background), any pay gap could hardly be attributed to gender discrimination — some salaries "favor" women while others "favor" men. In fact, an apples-to-apples Census Bureau statistic averaging single, childless, 20-something men and women in metropolitan areas show that women earn 8% more than males.[69]

In spite of the facts showing that "equal pay" is the law and in effect (though situations in which it is not practiced should be recognized as isolated cases of discrimination and reconciled), we understand that obstacles remain. This gets in the way of some women reaching their full academic or professional potential, and thereby skews down a sweeping female salary average. Beyond superficially addressing the outcome of these obstacles, we want to empower girls and young women to make strong decisions for themselves to overcome any obstacles they may face (e.g., peer pressure). We want to encourage girls from a young age to take an interest in all studies and professions, including those which are typically male-dominated or "nerdier" (e.g., math and sciences), and happen to also be higher-paying. We believe mindful educational approaches, positive role models, and participation in competitive activities are some ways to naturally and fundamentally — not bureaucratically — influence this issue.

Given the fact that equal pay is already federally protected, the federal government should not continue to enact more programs

---

[69]   http://www.aei.org/publication/the-case-against-the-paycheck-fairness-act/#mbl

or salary-related policies to "fix" the factually incorrect (yet often politicized) "epidemic" of gender-based pay discrimination. Consistent with conservative principles, we believe government intervention here is ineffective and unfair to Americans, both male *and* female. Outside of consequences for clear violations of the existing law (as should be under any other law), government scrutiny and meddling in the matter, especially from the federal level, inevitably create unintended consequences such as arbitrary investigations and reverse discrimination.

While liberal new-wave feminists may still blame misogynistic pressures (see Feminism section) for any pay variation, there is concrete evidence showing that nondiscriminatory, largely self-selecting factors lower the *overall* average of women's earnings. Nevertheless, a relentless pursuit to claim sweeping female pay discrimination provokes unproductive emotions of victimization, as well as diminishes the gravity of claims where gender discrimination does at times occur. The propaganda seems most effective in blaming and pitting one faction against another (e.g., Republican-Democrat, man-woman, misogynist-"feminist") than actually empowering females with opportunities to equally consider financially favorable educational and career options. As we see it, careers and subsequent salary decisions made by women (as with men) should be a matter of professional "pro-choice": we want to independently and prudently choose our own career path and work-life balance.

Feminism

Liberal Accusation: You are not a feminist.

BHC Counter: I am a feminist in every sense of the word. I believe women have rights to political, social, and economic opportunities equal to men.[70] My conservative principles, in particular equality, are completely aligned with feminism. After all, the Republican Party's members spearheaded the American feminist movement in the late 1800s and early 1900s. Republican women such as Susan B. Anthony led suffragists to press the nation to recognize a woman's right to vote (see Civil Rights section), securing women's participation in politics and government. In addition to equal rights, I believe women have equal capabilities to achieve. I view liberal accusations of blame (e.g., toward men, conservatives) and government dependency as anti-feminist, as these ultimately weaken society's perception of women as strong, capable, and independent.

Since the original feminist movement led by the suffragists, the meaning of feminism took a turn in the 1960s. Far-left liberals created the "Women's Liberation" movement and effectively altered feminism to reflect their radical mission. "New-wave" feminists also inspired a kind of female empowerment, but their version of empowerment involved ideals extraneous to the heart of pure feminism. Free-wheeling sexuality and abortion (it's nice having it both ways), as well as resentment towards males and scornful rejection of "traditional" gender roles, are examples of ideals championed by new-wave feminists. We respect everyone's right to free speech and thought, but we do not identify with the priorities of new-wave feminism — our disagreement has them categorizing us as misogynists.

Under new-wave feminism, traditionally female roles like full-time mother connote an unfavorable stereotype: the 1950s subservient housewife who is a victim of sexism and perpetuates

---

70   http://www.oxforddictionaries.com/us/definition/american_english/feminism

patriarchal American society. To the contrary, we believe the full-time mom plays a crucial role in society, one equal to that of a working mom. We celebrate any dedicated mother's prudent decision on how to live her life with the best interest of her children in mind. New-wave feminists should agree with us here, as this is a very "pro-choice" perspective on this matter.

In spite of what many liberals might want women voters to believe, conservative women and men have worked and fought for women's social, political, and economic opportunities to be equal to those of men's. Moreover, we believe feminism should not stop at our shores. While new-wave feminists continue to provoke questionable claims of sweeping injustices in the U.S., we prefer to prioritize the focus on leveraging the feminist qualities of the U.S. to motivate much-needed feminism (in the original sense of the word) around the world. A number of countries continue to not only deny women's rights but also commit unimaginable atrocities against women and young girls.[71] Conservatives are feminists domestically and abroad, then and now, and we will always believe in equal rights, respect, education, choice, and freedoms for women.

Safety

Conservatives find that assurances of safety are critical to the relevance of every other political issue, and therefore arguably hold it a high priority. We recognize that if we are not safe, personally or publically, then we inherently cannot be free. Safety gives us freedom, which affords us the ability to pursue

---

71   http://www.nytimes.com/2002/11/09/international/
        middleeast/09FPRO.html

goals, speak out, be who we are, go where we desire. Without the confidence that we can live safely and therefore freely, all of the debated social and fiscal issues, from the significant to the seemingly mundane, become irrelevant. As President Reagan stated, "If we don't have security, we'll have no need for social programs."[72]

Gun Control

Liberal Accusation: You must be a belligerent, gun-toting, trigger-happy NRA member.

BHC Counter: This depiction in no way characterizes me. I do, however, believe that the constitutional right to bear arms is reasonable and appropriate when responsibly upheld. An American citizen should be allowed to exercise this right in the interest of personal safety, under the condition that he or she passes necessary background checks in the interest of public safety. Further, I believe the liberal support of a gun ban as the solution to gun violence is impractical given the already-set precedent of gun ownership. To expect that all civilian guns (approximately 300 million[73]) will be relinquished upon a government-mandated ban is quite naive. In such a scenario, as the ominous adage goes, "If guns are outlawed, only outlaws will have guns." As part of my belief in the importance of the right to bear arms, I support strengthening the efficacy of background checks and safety regulations. If the right to bear arms intends to protect, background checks do the same, as

---

72   http://www.nationalreview.com/article/419229/ronald-reagan-liberal-myths-debunked

73   https://www.washingtonpost.com/news/wonk/wp/2015/10/05/guns-in-the-united-states-one-for-every-man-woman-and-child-and-then-some/

they help prevent the mentally unfit and people of ill-will from obtaining guns.

Conservatives believe registered and responsible people have a right to protect themselves and others around them with a firearm when faced with a life-threatening situation. Our Founding Fathers understood the importance of self-protection, which is very much in line with their general belief in a nation enabling its citizens to be self-empowered and self-reliant to every reasonable extent. The unfortunate and timeless truth is that life-threatening situations can become a reality at any given time. The Second Amendment was drafted because peace and order can never be guaranteed — especially not by government. A police department can help enforce peace and order, but in an instantaneous threatening situation, the police can only play a delayed and reactive role upon receiving a call for help.

Liberals generally believe that a ban on civilian gun ownership, which would require a repeal of the Second Amendment, is the appropriate solution to gun violence. This belief disregards the key fact that the majority of gun violence is committed with illegal guns or illegally obtained guns. The unintended consequences of a ban on legal civilian gun ownership would not prevent the continued trafficking of illegal guns, leaving the law-abiding citizen unable to protect himself or herself. A U.S. Department of Justice survey of state prison inmates found that less than 12% of criminals who committed gun-related crimes obtained their firearms from a legally recognized accountable venue.[74] As a proxy for illegal gun activity, we recognize that narcotics continue to be trafficked and used in spite of serious

---

[74]   http://www.bjs.gov/content/pub/pdf/fv9311.pdf

federal bans; but unlike narcotics, guns (legally handled) can and have been used to protect lives.

The National Rifle Association (NRA), famously *and* infamously known for its support of the right to private gun ownership, has become rhetorically synonymous with conservatism. While we appreciate the idea that the NRA defends the Second Amendment *and* understands a degree of conditional background checks must be met[75] (though we see that current checks in place need systematic improvements), we do not necessarily share the same passionate affinity for firearms. Hypothetically speaking, even if NRA members were exclusively registered Republicans, NRA membership would make up less than 15% of all registered Republicans.[76][77] This is a clear minority of the party's population, which is surprising given media portrayal and subsequent public perception that the GOP *is* the NRA. However, we are not all gun-brandishing cowboys, just as liberals are not all drugged-out hippies.

As with many political issues, statistics and anecdotes exist in support of both sides of the gun-control debate. Arriving at an absolute political position based on the mounds of available data could leave an objective analysis at a standstill. As a result, left-leaning people are preconditioned to reference left-leaning research by anti-gun advocates widely disseminated by mainstream media. On the other hand, conservative-minded people are more likely to note statistics and resources which

---

[75]   http://www.politico.com/story/2015/08/nra-supported-background-gun-check-john-cornyn-121035

[76]   http://www.pewresearch.org/fact-tank/2014/04/24/5-facts-about-the-nra-and-guns-in-america/

[77]   http://2012election.procon.org/view.resource.php?resourceID=004483

support the Second Amendment. For example, research conducted by Professor John Lott of the University of Chicago shows stricter gun laws (as in cities like Chicago) actually correlates with more gun crimes and murders.[78] He has found a striking pattern in which places under civilian gun restrictions seemingly invite criminal gunmen. Criminals are aware of areas in which bystanders are unarmed, and therefore know they will face less resistance against committing acts of violence.[79]

So for a variety of constitutional and practical reasons, conservatives believe it is important to preserve our right to self-protect (per our principle of self-reliance), as the alternatives do not offer promising or timely protections. We want government to focus on reducing gun violence not by condemning the Second Amendment, but rather through efforts ensuring responsible ownership and safe use of guns. For instance, we would support banning the sale of any gun without a background check, as well as improving the efficacy and thoroughness of background checks. Reports have shockingly revealed that millions of people barred by federal law from purchasing guns are never added to the federal background check system because of government unaccountability.[80] The reality that it is difficult enough for government to tackle responsible management of these lists further confirms our hunch that government-mandated gun bans would not be responsibly upheld.

---

[78] http://www.chicagotribune.com/news/opinion/commentary/ct-mall-of-america-terrorist-threat-perspec-0225-20150224-story.html

[79] http://www.forbes.com/sites/larrybell/2013/05/14/disarming-realities-as-gun-sales-soar-gun-crimes-plummet/

[80] http://www.huffingtonpost.com/2011/11/14/gun-check-system-misses-millions_n_1093899.html

Policing

Liberal Accusation: You don't believe police brutality is an epidemic which must be stopped.

BHC Counter: I agree there have been cases in which a police officer disgracefully and brutally handled a suspect. Some of these cases ended tragically and, as a conservative who stands by the importance of accountability, I believe those specific officers ought to face severe consequences. Nevertheless, given the nearly 1 million police officers serving our communities and the hundreds of thousands of daily 911 calls answered in every community, the recent denigration of law enforcement professionals as a whole is unwarranted and shameful. The sweeping backlash against admirable police officers is unjust and, more importantly, it is unconstructive (often destructive) to the goal of safer communities.

To achieve improved policing, healthier police-citizen relationships, and ultimately safer communities, there needs to be honest communication in *both* directions (i.e., the police officers and the community members). Our unequivocal respect for the general police force does not blind us to the fact that some individual officers have done wrong. Given that police officers are granted rights and allowances not applicable to civilians, they are automatically held to higher standards of responsibility and expectations. Improved training protocols, "community" policing practices (i.e., positive involvement in the community other than when called on for help), and body camera-equipped officers are some ideas which could sustainably improve policing for the officers and ultimately for the communities.

While much of the responsibility to improve policing falls on the department and its officers, the broader solution also requires broader community examination — for instance, family structure, education, job opportunities, and morals. Civilian citizens are the fundamental components which make a community safe, with the police department merely serving as a support system for that community's safety. A community looking only at the wrongs of its police needs to look at itself and how elements unrelated to law enforcement impact its citizens and consequently interaction with officers.

Conservatives highly respect police officers for their work in serving and protecting the public in spite of the risks inherent to their job. Few professionals (including those of military and firefighting) join police officers in routinely putting his or her life at risk for the good of the larger population. Just as we see police brutality as unjust, disgraceful, and tragic, conservatives lament the injustice, disgrace, and tragedy involving injured or murdered police officers. Unfortunately, not everyone sees it both ways. In our relentless vision of equality for all, it is difficult for us not to recognize the lack of demonstrations and media coverage in response to a murdered police officer (or for that matter a murdered black person at the hands of a black civilian). The uproars, protests, marches, vigils, and media scrutiny in response to unlawful (or even *allegedly* unlawful) police handling of a black citizen are far more passionate than that of the response heard when the victim is a police officer (including those of white, black, Asian, and Hispanic backgrounds).

The unjust treatment against the overall admirable institution of law enforcement is not only unfair to police officers but it is also unsafe for communities which are most at-risk. Police officers are consciously and subconsciously more reluctant to perform their duties, as they are very aware of the heightened (as well as biased) scrutiny and violence they face on a given day in the post-Ferguson, Missouri, policing era (also known as "The Ferguson Effect").[81] Any public opinion of a wrongfully forceful attempt to self-protect or keep the streets safe can easily result in accusations of police brutality and lead to reputational damage if not career-ending consequences. This is not worth the risk for an individual police officer and especially not for the family he or she supports. FBI Director James Comey believes that police restraint in the wake of this criticism is at least partly to blame for the surge in violent crimes in cities.[82]

Given liberals' passion for asserting the fact that Islamic terrorist extremists do not define Muslims and similarly rioters do not represent protesters (to which we agree with both), it is curious to us why liberals do not apply the same rationale in favor of police departments (see Applicable Extremism section). It is clear that many of them (e.g., Black Lives Matter demonstrators) view police brutality simply as today's "policing." But the truth is that a very marginal number of unnecessarily forceful or negligent officers (certainly not of epidemic-like proportion) do not define law enforcement and do not represent police. In contrast, they represent abhorrent exceptions to the rule and should be stripped of their badges. Given media selection and sensationalism focused on the exceptions, it is easy to take real police presence, accessibility, and protection for granted. The media are not as interested in covering stories when police act heroically or, in other words, just do their job.

---

81   http://nypost.com/2014/10/14/the-ferguson-effect-a-cops-eye-view/
82   http://www.cnn.com/2015/10/26/politics/fbi-comey-crime-police/

Profiling

Liberal Accusation: You believe it's okay to judge someone based on appearance or by their associations.

BHC Counter: I believe that law enforcement is required for the sake of public safety to make judgments (not convictions) based on criminal patterns or witness descriptions involving physical or behavioral characteristics — otherwise known as profiling. The legal practice of profiling provides an effective method for investigators and officers to locate a criminal. Profiles lead to a suspect, a person believed to be responsible for a crime based on an idea or impression of the truth without certain proof[83] but who is considered innocent until proven guilty. Upon further investigation of the profiled suspect, he or she is either released or put on trial, where a verdict is made. That said, I also firmly believe that any practice disguised as profiling which actually violates an individual's rights without reasonable suspicion is corrupt and warrants consequences.

Conservatives prioritize the individual and individual rights; however, there are times when collective interest in public safety and administration of justice may come into conflict with the individual (e.g., warrants; see Surveillance section). As it relates to profiling, we believe law enforcement should be allowed to make determinations of suspects based on their expert knowledge, professional experience, and legitimate tips. For instance, when a series of crimes has been committed

---

83   http://www.oxforddictionaries.com/us/definition/american_english/
        suspect

by various criminals all sharing common traits (these traits comprise the "profile"), universal reasoning implies a greater likelihood that a subsequent comparable crime was committed by someone fitting that profile. Law enforcement uses profile information not only to catch criminals but also to prevent future violence and stop criminal recruitment, especially within at-risk communities. Logic like this seems rational; however, the debate arises when emotion suppresses logic — when an individual or particular group feels a profile implies racial or ethnic discrimination. But when public safety is at risk, we generally believe facts, statistics, and probabilities should outweigh emotion.

Profiling has recently become a particularly controversial political issue in spite of the fact that it has been a recognized and effective law enforcement practice here for over a century. Duration alone is not what justifies it. Rather, over this time various criminal activities have been eliminated through profiling practices — proving time and again the efficacy of profiling. During the early-to-mid 20th century, for example, certain demographic groups were profiled by law enforcement. One such notable group of the time included Italian-Americans, given associations with an organized crime syndicate known as the Mafia. Due largely to the use of profiling practices, many of these criminal organizations of the past are now just that — a thing of the past.

Profiles are generated according to the criminal and threatening circumstances of the period. In more recent times, the same statistical-based reasoning brings law enforcement to profile suspects of other traits — most controversially including those within at-risk black and Muslim communities. Just as in times past, profiling strategies help to enable law enforcement to locate and apprehend suspects, thereby preventing threatening and dangerous activity, ultimately saving lives. In many cases the lives saved are of similar race or ethnicity to the profiled perpetrators. However, unlike in times past, law enforcement has been vehemently criticized by some liberals over profiling, alleging racism disguised as profiling. Any alleged isolated instances should be dealt with seriously and severely, but it should not deter from upholding profiling strategy as the effective law enforcement tool it is.

Incarceration

Liberal Accusation: Your support for mass incarceration unjustly punishes the black and Hispanic minority populations.

BHC Counter: I believe that any person, regardless of color, creed, or class, who breaks the law ought to face appropriate consequences. Conviction, sentencing, and incarceration of the accused ought to be justly determined as written by law, cognizant of the criminal's authentic mental state, and blind to the criminal's racial, ethnic, or socioeconomic background. This position not only serves the purposes of deterring a potential offender, punishing the convicted, and delivering justice to the victim, but also enhancing public safety more broadly. At the same time, I believe that attention needs to focus on reforming the current incarceration system in order to make a more just, effective, and efficient system, particularly as it relates to minor nonviolent criminal incarceration.

The suggestion that the Republican Party has a racist agenda in support of mass incarceration is a lie. Moreover, it is counterproductive to finding an honest solution to disproportionate minority incarceration and overall flaws within the criminal justice system. Ironic to such racist accusations against the Right is the history of the mass incarceration wave. The 1994 crime bill which catalyzed mass incarceration was actually passed by then-President Bill Clinton. He later admitted that the bipartisan crime bill he signed into law worsened the nation's criminal justice system by increasing prison sentences. He now believes the law "cast too wide a net and we had too many people in prison... putting so many people in prison that there wasn't enough money left to educate them, train them for new jobs, and increase the chances when they came out so they could live productive lives" — a sentiment that conservatives can certainly support. In a later statement he added, "The good news is we had the biggest drop in crime in history. The bad news is we had a lot people who were locked up, who were minor actors, for way too long." Clinton ultimately believes the results of his law were mixed, at best.[84] As with virtually all policy issues, a balance must be struck; in this case, one which rectifies unreasonable incarceration while maintaining the consequence of incarceration as a means to deter and punish crime.

As we look forward to and work towards the day when our justice system will truly be blind, we understand the unfortunate present-day reality that many convictions and sentencings are influenced (both favorably and unfavorably to the accused) by wealth and by race — arguably working in favor of a celebrity defendant like O.J. Simpson and leaving poor and minority defendants at a grave disadvantage. Unjustly applied treatment, convictions, and sentences are plainly unconstitutional (see Civil Rights section), specifically with regard to equality and

---

84   http://www.cnn.com/2015/07/15/politics/bill-clinton-1994-crime-bill/

due process. Such individuals subsequently find themselves figuratively and literally imprisoned by a criminal justice system which, notwithstanding the existence of racial bias, appears to have been poorly planned. Where biased treatment exists, focus should be on disciplining or displacing officials who participate in discriminatory practices *clearly* evidenced by conduct patterns or other indications.

Beyond a partisan-blaming or race-based matter, we believe the incarceration problem ought to be examined from the broader criminal justice system. For one, disproportionate and unnecessarily extensive prison sentences for minor offenses can have unintended consequences detrimental to the individual (e.g., personal opportunity cost) and to the larger society (e.g., taxpayer dollars). Where this exists, productive debate should focus on legislative reforms. With now decades-worth of relevant incarceration data and consideration of longer-term effects on the individual and society, lawmakers can better identify appropriate sentence terms which appropriately fit the crime (e.g., marijuana offenses). Additionally, correctional facilities which fail to actually correct when possible (as evidenced primarily by high criminal relapse, also known as recidivism) only run against the institution's true purpose. Where this fails, productive debate should focus on institutional administration reforms. For example, restructured inmate rehabilitation requirements and basic life-skills training in a transitional phase should be mandatory during the latter time of a prison sentence. An inmate's failure to show some potential or cooperation in this phase ought to result in an alternative disciplinary program — something other than allowing the criminal to live freely among an innocent community. However, an inmate's success in a transitional phase will prepare him or her for healthy integration back into society as a free individual. We believe that prisons are not just temporary residences for convicted criminals serving time; rather, prisons should also function as a disciplinary and truly *correctional* facility to enable prisoners to help themselves as well as the communities to which they will eventually return.

We view appropriately applied and administered incarceration as a necessary institution for the purpose of law and order. And with proper reform efforts, there is the potential to fundamentally improve the mind-set and lives of once-incarcerated individuals, in particular those guilty of minor nonviolent offenses. As evidenced by post-incarceration transition initiatives such as The Doe Fund's "Ready, Willing, & Able" program, the right approaches prove effective, with graduates securing skills, sobriety, a job, and a renewed sense of dignity.[85] From there the overall safety and well-being of those around them, including family, neighbors, community, and so on, will also be improved. Additionally, the economic benefits of properly reforming the incarceration system imply more efficiently allocated tax dollars. This would suggest incrementally more self-reliant citizens working and supporting themselves, their families, and their communities.

Capital Punishment

Liberal Accusation: "Eye for an eye" is a barbaric justification for the death penalty.

BHC Counter: I believe the death penalty is a just consequence for the utmost intentionally evil, horrific, homicidal crimes. I

---

85   http://www.doe.org/services_detail.cfm?programID=13

do not consider it a penalty founded solely by a biblical "eye for an eye" principle. Rather, I view it as grounded in practical intentions toward the goal of a safe and just society (e.g., through disincentives, consequences, accountability). While constitutional law of punishment proportionality (i.e., "the punishment must fit the crime") is rooted in the idea of "eye for an eye," it also serves as a form of severe disincentive for some would-be killers from committing the most severe form of crime. Additionally, the death penalty inherently guarantees the murderer cannot strike again (in prison or upon escape as we saw possible, for instance, with the New York and California maximum security prison breaks of five murderers over 2015 and 2016[86][87]).

Then-governor of Massachusetts, Mitt Romney, summarized this debate best: "On one side, there are some people who believe there are certain crimes that are so offensive... so reprehensible... so far beyond the bounds of civilized society that they demand the ultimate punishment. In the other camp are well-meaning people who believe that it is immoral for government to ever take a life. In the middle, I believe, are others who could support the death penalty if it is narrowly applied and contains the appropriate safeguards."[88] It is with this group in mind that we believe there are specific, rigorously-qualified, and "narrowly applied" times which call for the death penalty.

---

[86] http://www.usatoday.com/story/news/2015/07/04/prison-escapee-unfolded/29648113/

[87] http://www.usatoday.com/story/news/nation/2016/01/26/fresno-man-could-key-stunning-california-jailbreak/79337272/

[88] http://2012.republican-candidates.org/Romney/Capital-Punishment.php

The Left generally opposes capital punishment, arguing that it is immoral under any circumstance to take a life (it is ironic how the tables blindly turn against an unborn baby in the abortion debate). However, in a moral debate around justice, our moral compass operates with priority regard to the murdered innocent and their families (e.g., victims of the Boston Marathon bombers) and the justice they might seek. Morals also have us considering potential future victims saved by this ultimate sentencing of a cold-blooded murderer.

The opposition also believes capital punishment does not actually serve as a significant deterrent. Not surprisingly, there are studies supporting both sides of this argument. Still, in either case of significant or insignificant deterrent, if just one incremental would-be murderer changes his or her behavior in concern over facing the ultimate consequence, then that is at least one incremental innocent life saved. The likelihood of this scenario alone makes a legal consequence of capital punishment worth honestly considering.

Two other points commonly referenced to argue against capital punishment involve the exorbitant cost of death row and the absolute injustice of a wrongful execution. We agree with these very valid concerns, *especially* the latter. However, given the objectives of capital punishment, conservatives recognize these points as areas to reform rather than as cause for complete repeal. First, objecting to the costs of death row implies there is a price at which the death penalty is "worth it." Conservatives are always in full support of initiatives to streamline the expenditure of taxpayer dollars, as in this case involving death row — for instance, making public costs toward a convict's appeals process more efficient while of course maintaining due process.

The hardest-hitting argument against capital punishment is wrongful execution after realizing a false conviction. It is in everyone's best interest — that of the victim, our society, and most importantly the wrongfully convicted — to rigorously strengthen the criteria by which a death penalty may be applied. Reform could include more precise specifications on how eye witness or DNA evidence must be offered, accepted, and weighted for the death penalty to first be an *option* upon sentencing a mentally stable defendant. Given our core value of innocent life, we are only in full support of infallible capital punishment sentencing. To address the not uncommon accusation of hypocrisy with regard to our stance on capital punishment vis-à-vis abortion, the application of each is accepted on a limited, very specifically qualified basis.

We are not callous to the fact that this issue is wrought with moral dilemma, but we acknowledge that the moral dilemma goes in both directions of the debate. With this in mind, our strong beliefs in the efficacy of disincentives, a form of justice to many victims' families, and an absolute way to prevent a cold-blooded murderer from killing again have us favoring scrupulously applied capital punishment. As noted in a recent Gallup poll, "Moral acceptance may remain high [at 60%] even as the death penalty dwindles in actual application. There are times when Americans appear to unite behind a death penalty conviction — as in the case of the Boston Marathon bomber Dzhokhar Tsarnaev, and before him, Oklahoma City bomber Timothy McVeigh — and thus the average American might want the option preserved for such situations."[89]

---

[89]   http://www.gallup.com/poll/183503/americans-continue-say-death-penalty-morally.aspx

Culture

Culture in the context of the United States relates to a variety of practices and can been seen in many forms. Throughout our nation's unique patchwork of ethnicities, races, and religions, conservatives understand the underlying commonality which binds us is that we are all American. Even as each of us maintains our individual traditions, activities, and tastes, we or our families before us came to the U.S. for a common reason: to be free and to live as described by our Founding Fathers in the late 1700s. Embracing this thought is not only a patriotic sentiment but a practical one, as well. The following sections cover a range of cultural-turned-political topics, from religious to social to behavioral. Conservatives believe that current controversies involving cultural issues contribute to the breakdown of other matters dividing our country today. In kind we believe a restructuring of how Americans view these cultural issues could help in easing the divisiveness.

American Exceptionalism

Liberal Accusation: Your belief in American exceptionalism is arrogant and close-minded.

BHC Counter: While even my liberal friends would attest to the fact that I am not arrogant or close-minded, I am proud of the U.S. and the principles for which it stands. I view our nation's founding principles as unique on the international stage, and that is what makes our country unusually excellent — in other words, *exceptional*. No other country begins one of its supreme governing documents by headlining unalienable rights of life, liberty, and the pursuit of happiness. Recognition of our nation's exceptional qualities makes for healthy patriotism and solidarity (this is not the same as arrogance). This in turn puts us in a more respectable position on the world stage, since we must respect ourselves if we want others to respect us.

Many liberals believe that touting American exceptionalism is conceited or just view it as untrue. The many faults they see still plaguing our country, their mistaken association of patriotism with chauvinism, or a general aversion to competition which might imply one country is "better" than another are some reasons for their opinion. There are a few key points that these liberal critics overlook. For one, patriotism does not exclude the ability to have sincere respect for other countries. Second, "exceptionalism" does not imply "perfect" — we don't believe our country is perfect. We do not tout American perfection but rather American exceptionalism. Since 1776 we have become more exceptional, largely credited to continuously self-reflecting and self-correcting, with an objective to become as close to the stated American ideal as possible. The reality is that the stated ideal will never be unanimously agreed upon in a democracy, but that does make for a "perfect" democracy.

The bottom line is we believe Americans have a right and are encouraged to own a sense of patriotism. As conservatives we are inclined to believe that our country is the best; however, our patriotism does not diminish our respect for other nations, their patriotism, and their beliefs that they are the best (we are happy to adopt their best practices where appropriate). But as Americans we can be proud of our country for the unique story and qualities which motivated its founding and all of its achievements to follow. Many of these admirable qualities, which have enabled the U.S. to be exceptional for its citizens as well as for the world, are addressed throughout the book. There is no other country on the planet which has attracted and continues to attract as many immigrants as has the U.S. Although not perfect, our country must be doing something exceptional.

Political Correctness

Liberal Accusation: That's politically incorrect. (*In response to just about anything conservative-minded*)

BHC Counter: You are absolutely right — some of what I think and say is not deemed politically correct according to liberal-controlled figurative "PC police." However, my thoughts and words are also not pander, not disrespectful, and not rhetoric. Sometimes honesty and facts can come into conflict with PC, but they maintain decency, positive purpose, and respect. I believe all people should demonstrate at least a basic level of common courtesy towards others; however, I find today's politically correct environment as more suitable for satirizing a comically pitiful hypersensitive PC environment than for the intention of sparing hurt feelings. From a policy standpoint, PC acts as an obstacle in identifying and then facing the root of an issue. Additionally, PC pressures rejection of certain words and references, which censors basic practice of free speech.

Sensitivity and courtesy can play an important role in the way diplomatic and effective communication is delivered. However, conservatives see the emotionally sensitive PC culture as a trend spinning out of control. If diplomacy is being thoughtful about how to effectively phrase a thought, then political correctness is diplomatic extremism. We all know that extremism of any kind spoils true intent and has consequences — this is no exception. PC fits the bill of fanatical religion given a cult-like following and severe judgments against those who do not observe. It is also disconcerting that the rules of PC vary depending on who you are and to whom you are speaking. Being politically correct today involves suppressions, restrictions, and double standards.

There are quite a few areas regulated by the PC police. These regulations can put pressure on innocuous everyday nonevents, to more substantial goal-oriented discussions. In an everyday situation, for example, political correctness elicits hesitation and second-guessing around word choices (expletives and derogatory terms aside) over fear of inadvertently *sounding* offensive (but not *actually saying* anything offensive): Is it inappropriate to relevantly reference *certain* ethnic descriptions? What is the appropriate way to describe a person's race? According to PC, "white" seems fair game for all; "Oriental" is now deemed un-PC, so is it okay to refer to someone as "Asian" or must this be qualified with "Asian-[American]"? In the same vein, is "black" or "African-[American]" more appropriate? Or is it better to act as though I don't notice altogether? It seems *whispering* a racial, ethnic, or religious description implies prejudice, but would plainly stating it be perceived inappropriately? Ironically, whispering indicates sensitivity to the matter, though the very act of *whispering* a certain characteristic implies an element of discomfort, which is in another way "racist." It seems PC philosophy demands that society literally act as if blind to a person's ethnic or cultural characteristics to prove rejection of racism and prejudice.

The PC police are also vigilant in the more significant realm of policy and solutions-oriented discussion. As it relates to anything from race and ethnicity, to gender and sexual orientation, and so on, a politically correct world inequitably dictates what can and cannot be said. For instance, Larry Summers, former president of Harvard University, unpleasantly experienced PC judgments when he spoke at a conference addressing gender representation in math and science, and specifically that women are underrepresented in these fields. We find it obvious that this was not addressed with indifferent rhetoric, with the intent of leaving the matter status quo. Rather, in an effort to open dialogue in order to identify solutions, he went on to reference a researched hypothesis in which "innate" differences between men and women were cited as a possible factor behind female underrepresentation.[90] A female professor in the audience was flustered by the mention of Summers' crass, sexist (read: politically incorrect) suggestion[91]—which ironically only played into another stereotype of women innately being more emotional and sensitive than men. She subsequently publicized Summers' "offensive" statement to the media. Others echoed this sentiment, feeling that female underrepresentation is yet another result of societal misogyny. The story elicited national media scrutiny. Subsequent to the PR frenzy, Summers received a vote of no confidence in his leadership.[92] In our opinion, some of these hypersensitive sentiments, especially on college campuses, ought to be replaced with real world rationality and resilience.

From our perspective, if gender-based "innate differences" are in fact the reason behind female underrepresentation in particular fields then this should be made known. With honest awareness, suitable adjustments can be made (e.g., via teaching styles, early stage awareness) to achieve acceptable female representation, or at least to motivate young girls to not

---

[90]   http://www.thecrimson.com/article/2005/1/14/summers-comments-on-women-and-science/

[91]   http://www.washingtonpost.com/wp-dyn/articles/A19181-2005Jan18.html

[92]   http://www.thecrimson.com/article/2005/3/15/lack-of-confidence-in-a-sharp/

forsake interest in traditionally male-dominated fields. Note in the event that subsequent studies show "innate differences" is categorically *not* a factor, then simply rule that out and investigate further. Under the ruling of PC, all the sensitive thought put into selection of words and phrasing takes away from the effective thought put into real action; it also tries to prevent asking the necessary (and possibly uncomfortable) probing questions in the first place. As we see it, the discriminatory PC climate is even clearer when considering a reverse scenario: would it have been politically incorrect and offensively received if President Summers stated a hypothesis that men are innately more violent than women? We think not.

Generally speaking, conservative-minded approaches to problem-solving of any kind require awareness of the root cause of an issue, as politically incorrect as it might sound, if there is intent to truly fix the issue. We find it critical to consider, identify, and address basic matters attributable to an individual or a group of individuals (consistent with our beliefs in accountability and personal responsibility). This can, of course, conflict with the conveniences of a politically correct approach, as personal responsibility is tougher to accept than a PC technique of placing blame on external factors (e.g., institutionalized discrimination) influencing unfavorable personal choices or situations.

We realize that elements of sexism, racism, and social biases do exist and can pose obstacles. These obstacles, verbal and otherwise, are not to be confused with being politically *in*correct. Rather, in the spirit of "un-PC", we also call this out like it is — discrimination. Fortunately, today's realities widely condemn discrimination, embrace diversity, inspire tolerance, and legally protect civil rights. So in tandem with a recognition of institutionalized means which *encourage* society to be one of equality and respect, we passionately believe in promoting a culture in which the individual understands he or she is in control of his or her own destiny — she can become a scientist, he can pursue higher education — without relying on the debilitating PC crutch of blaming externalities for difficult personal circumstances.

We believe an honest and perhaps "politically incorrect" method serves as an effective approach to improving an individual's circumstance as well as defeating negative generalizations which may unfairly burden an individual. Generalizations, and to a degree stereotypes, are manifested basically from objective statistics and probabilities based on collective instances of reality (e.g., men generally are physically stronger than women, and women generally are emotionally smarter than men). These can have negative and positive associations. Generalizations are not to be confused with misogynistic or derogatory statements, which are specifically motivated by negativity and based on prejudice, ignorance, or ill will. We view legitimate generalizations not as something to shy away from but rather as something which can be harnessed and used productively; for instance, to turn a negative generalization into a positive one, or to take a positive generalization and apply qualities about it elsewhere. Hopefully as society tires of self-righteous PC attitudes where thoughts, statements, and generalizations are condemned and censored, attention can be redirected toward opportunities for open discussions with the purpose of coming to honest solutions.

Immigration

Liberal Accusation: You are anti-immigration.

BHC Counter: I wholeheartedly support immigration from an ideological standpoint as well as from a personal perspective. Some of the most patriotic and inspirational people I know are immigrants. I view liberals' false accusation that conservatives oppose immigration as one of the most deceitfully spun lies spread in politics. To be clear, I do not support *illegal* immigration, with the critical word being illegal — this is absolutely no different than my stance on anything illegal (don't do it, otherwise face the consequences if caught). I find the distinction between immigration versus *illegal* immigration analogous to parking versus *illegal* parking: the act of parking is completely acceptable, commonplace, often necessary; however, *illegal* parking, especially in high frequencies and in dangerous situations, creates disorder and risk to everyone. Immigration laws are intended to protect everyone, not just American citizens, who are legally in the U.S. However, it has become evident that current laws and processes around immigration are impractical, and I believe our government needs to democratically reform current policies.

Conservatives are proud that our country is a nation of immigrants. The spirit, productivity, and character which immigrants bring with them have helped make the United States what it is, and continue to do so. We are also proud that our country is a nation of laws and order, which brings many immigrants here in the first place. We believe the laws should be respected, or otherwise democratically amended if deemed flawed. In the U.S., the law is intended to apply to everyone, including politicians, everyday citizens, visitors, and immigrants.

Many liberals speak of immigration and illegal immigration (if they even mention the *illegal* aspect at all) as a distinction without a difference. However, there is an explicit difference, one centered on legality. Our country was founded on the rule of law, so this difference is particularly significant. Nevertheless, liberals have slanderously labeled conservatives as fascist and racist, as they misrepresent our views on what they generalize as "immigration." They seem to altogether ignore the legalities and complexities of the issue. The truth is that our regard for the "lawful" element is central to this debate. We recognize that the laws which determine legal versus illegal immigration (the same laws which require the protocol of "checking-in" since the immigration waves at Ellis Island) were *not* passed to maintain a xenophobic system to keep foreigners out; rather, they were made to uphold security and order.

For the purposes of security and planning, foreign entry into the U.S. today requires proof of identity, legitimacy via passport, and sometimes a visa. Obtaining a green card and subsequently U.S. citizenship requires a process involving filing an application, background checks, an interview, and a test. This aims to ensure that all people in the U.S. — native, naturalized, and temporary — live within a secure and well-planned society. Immigrant entry or overstay which disregards these procedural laws constitutes illegal activity, and like anything illegal, consequences ought to follow. We do not believe that people who are here from other countries should be an exception to this. Such an immigration system is not unique to the U.S. All civilized nations wishing to uphold order require similar entry process and enforcement.

Conservatives and liberals agree that the current immigration system has much room for improvement but we differ on what makes reform for the better. Conservatives want to reform immigration laws to facilitate moral, productive, law-abiding foreigners looking to realize an American dream. At the same time, we want to prevent illegal, dangerous, and suspicious entries into the U.S. This requires a tough but necessary balance. We believe sustainable reform requires fortifying border controls and advancing comprehensive background check systems. With international travelers regularly undergoing TSA scrutiny and Homeland Security controls in airports, controls along our borders should be equally tight. Borders which are recognized as being especially subject to illegal activity ought to be given extra attention.

We believe reform measures should not only be focused on the part of the immigrant. For instance, a conservative-minded means of deterring illegal immigration involves enforcing penalties on U.S. employers who hire undocumented illegal immigrant workers. We understand that many illegal immigrants come here for job opportunities, and we want to incentivize these workers to take the legal approach. Legal entry is mutually beneficial to the U.S. and to immigrants, as this will set up immigrants-turned-citizens or legal residents to realize a true American life of freedom and opportunity (and taxes!). We believe that a U.S. employer who breaks the law by inviting susceptible illegal immigrants to also break the law should be penalized.

Without proper reforms, vulnerabilities remain tempting opportunities for those with a will to illegally take advantage. While the logistics of the immigration system are in place primarily for the sake of structural law and order, inherent to this is security. For the most dangerous scenarios, we view comprehensive immigration control measures as critical to countering grave realities of the relatively very few but disproportionately very destructive foreign-based criminals, drug smugglers, human traffickers, and infiltrating terrorists (see National Security section). Though the vast majority of illegal immigrants originate from Latin America,[93] threats can originate from anywhere around the world to exploit the porous southern border of the U.S. Nevertheless, defensive measures such as those focused on border security and background checks have been criticized by liberals for being un-American, unwelcoming, excessive, and discriminatory against foreigners. Our priority concern is not for the impression made at the border, but rather it is for the need to guarantee security for all who are legally here and wish to legally come here. This includes native citizens, naturalized citizens, immigrants, refugees, and visitors. Furthermore, with just about every country in the world requiring its own appropriate processes for legal entry, established immigration systems for the purpose of domestic accountability also facilitate global security via international cooperation.

In addition to law, order, and security, a respected immigration policy helps to preserve accountable operations of commonplace societal matters (e.g., education, health care). Conservatives understand the inconvenient reality that U.S. resources are not infinite; so just like a personal budget, a household, or a business, a society's resources (including structural, human, and fiscal) are limited at any given point in time. It is unfortunately infeasible for a country with one-third of its citizens presently receiving some type of public assistance[94] and with many of its young citizens subjected to a broken

---

[93]   http://www.npr.org/templates/story/story.php?storyId=4703307

[94]   http://www.census.gov/programs-surveys/sipp/publications/tables/hsehld-char.html

public education system to appropriately support itself and an immeasurable number of illegal immigrants who want to be here at their discretion. With serious domestic troubles (e.g., poverty, hunger) existing in the U.S. as it is, spreading already meager public resources even thinner among a hundred million Americans plus an indefinite number more would be of no real support to anyone in need. Largely for this reason our nation has in place a legal immigration process — one which can and should be improved — which looks to balance practicing domestic responsibility with welcoming law-abiding and hard-working immigrants.

In spite of the inability of the U.S., or any country for that matter, to responsibly admit an unlimited number of immigrants, we do not and will not turn a blind eye to deprived foreign citizens. Our government and private charities allocate a significant amount of taxpayer and private money to help people of other nations. Mexico, for example, receives hundreds of millions of dollars annually.[95] However, hundreds of thousands of Mexicans each year continue to flee poverty and violence, implying a structural problem within Mexico — one which is obviously not being solved by throwing money at its government. A conservative-minded solution would involve providing conditional and directed funding to discourage corruption and guarantee optimal humanitarian impact — that is, keeping recipient governments accountable. With regard to more critical refugee scenarios, we support the U.S. for its long-standing will to extend itself as a beacon of hope. Even in foreign refugee situations where the U.S. is potentially subjected to terrorist infiltration (such as the ISIS terrorist in the November 2015

---

[95]   http://us-foreign-aid.insidegov.com/q/112/1590/How-much-money-does-the-U-S-give-to-Mexico

Paris attack who entered the EU as a faux Syrian refugee[96]), we believe sending assistance abroad is the best way to help refugees in trouble while protecting Americans' security at home. Conservatives understand that the most effective way for the U.S. to help disadvantaged global citizens is to fix the problem at the source of dysfunction, as taking everyone in is simply unsustainable and detrimental.

In contrast to our perspectives, liberals generally view a more open border, ever-accessible entry, and a nearly undiscerning admittance policy as representative of the American way. For instance, a liberal solution to the illegal immigration issue as it exists today supports amnesty, an official pardon for people having committed an illegal act. This allows illegal immigrants to circumvent the legal immigration process — a process with which 1 million law-abiding immigrants willingly comply each year.[97] We believe that weak borders and amnesty encourage illegal entry (not to mention snub law-abiding, citizenship-pending immigrants). This ultimately exacerbates the social and fiscal concerns of illegal immigration, as evidenced by the bipartisan 1986 amnesty program signed by then-President Reagan (who later reportedly regretted this decision because of these unintended consequences).[98] While idealized gestures and representations may suggest kindness, we believe true kindness is demonstrated by honest practices grounded in realistic solutions which offer long-term efficacy.

---

96   http://www.cnn.com/2015/11/15/europe/paris-attacks-passports/

97   http://www.politifact.com/florida/statements/2012/jun/20/marco-rubio/marco-rubio-says-us-admits-1-million-immigrants-ye/

98   http://humanevents.com/2006/12/13/reagan-would-not-repeat-amnesty-mistake/

Given practical sense and historical evidence, amnesty for the estimated 11 million illegal undocumented immigrants in the U.S.[99] is not at all a solution. Rather, a conservative-minded efficient approach to handling 11 million illegal immigrants already here includes plans such as allowing illegal immigrants to earn their way (e.g., through conditions and fines) to legal status. This approach aims to balance the impracticality of deportation in such great magnitude, with the importance of bringing illegal immigrants out of the shadows, while recognizing the principles of accountability and consequences. While logistical details are no doubt complex and up for debate, this type of plan illustrates conservatives' interest in achieving the appropriate balance of practicality, compassion, and equality (i.e., everyone must obey the law). A one-time program like this serves to reset the country's population in preparation for an honest, comprehensive plan to reform our country's immigration system and resolve illegal immigration issues.

Ultimately, we want to preserve the spirit of honest immigration, a precious component of what makes American society. We equally want to maintain safety and security for U.S. citizens, legal immigrants, and visitors. Immigrants come to the U.S. because of qualities enabled by our observance and enforcement of the rule of law. Everyone must be subject to the law, otherwise the exceptions become the rule — in which case law and order, a major motivating factor behind many immigrants' journey here, is lost.

Assimilation

Liberal Accusation: Assimilation is a fascist expectation.

---

[99]   http://www.dhs.gov/publication/estimates-unauthorized-immigrant-population-residing-united-states-january-2012

BHC Counter: I believe that American assimilation is an empowering expectation. To assimilate into American culture specifically implies that an immigrant and generations after can maintain their native culture while simultaneously integrating within their new, naturalized society. Boundless opportunities are available to anyone with the will to familiarize with basic ties which characterize American society. Respect for U.S. rule of law, the English language, and an industrious culture will pave the way for any citizen, native or naturalized, to achieve his or her fullest potential in the United States.

Contrary to what liberals prefer to acknowledge, conservatives are proud that we are a nation of immigrants. Our uniquely heterogeneous society is part of what makes the U.S. exceptional. We value citizens and residents who add to the cultural makeup of the U.S., and we embrace those who want to participate in and contribute to existing American culture (e.g., basic English, work ethic, tolerance). In other words, we see diversity and assimilation as very mutually inclusive in the American way of life.

An expectation of assimilation has become a political point of contention. Some liberals view assimilation has having fascist, xenophobic connotations. In contrast, conservatives view an appropriate degree of assimilation — not only in the U.S. but within any country — as a way to most effectively prosper in a new society. Not to mention, assimilation demonstrates a token of respect for that society.

A rudimentary level of assimilation involves a basic understanding of the national language. From a practical standpoint, an official unified language facilitates order and safety within a society. In the U.S., English can be critical in everyday as well as urgent scenarios. This includes understanding street signs to communicating medical emergencies. An official language is also the foundation of a structured and effective education system. English is not only a primary academic subject, but it is also the language in which all other subjects are taught. Language assimilation enables an individual to better achieve academic as well as socioeconomic success. Without language comprehension, communication barriers inhibit overall quality of life in any country. A glut of foreign language crutches (as seen in some municipalities) serves to facilitate non-English speaking citizens in the short-term but is ultimately detrimental to them in the long-term: socioeconomic statistics such as literacy rates, employment, and earnings potential suffer.[100] Fostering a culture in which verbal and literate understanding of the national language is encouraged and facilitated only strengthens an individual's ability to reach his or her fullest social and economic potential. This in turn strengthens our nation as a whole.

Religion

Liberal Accusation: You must be a devout Christian.

BHC Counter: I am not especially religious and I am not Christian. Nevertheless, I appreciate the historical fact that our country's founding was influenced by virtuous principles inspired by our Founders' Christian backgrounds. Like so many conservatives of various backgrounds, ranging from traditionally religious (Christian, Jewish, Muslim, etc.) to alternatively

---

[100]   http://www.wsj.com/articles/limited-english-limits-job-prospects-1411531262

spiritual to atheist, my personal beliefs are extraneous to my respect for the religious aspects of our nation's foundation. More significantly, I respect the basic right to religious freedom which allows all Americans to observe their own faiths as long as practices do not interfere with another individual's rights and safety. And especially given the vital role religion played in our nation's formation, I appreciate the Founders' modesty and forward thinking in establishing separation between church and state in the First Amendment of the Constitution.

Our Founding Fathers created this country with ideals including religious freedom and unalienable rights endowed by their Creator. These ideals, influenced by the Founders' primarily Protestant backgrounds, were identified as a basis for creating a better nation. The Protestant ethic emphasizes hard work, frugality, and diligence.[101] We believe these principles contributed to making the "American dream" a possibility to all and a reality to countless individuals throughout our history; as a result, millions of immigrants continue to be motivated to move to the U.S. (see Immigration section) — numbers far greater than that of any other nation on the planet.[102] Two centuries-worth of realized American dreams have led to our country's uniquely exceptional reputation.

The guarantee of religious freedoms and tolerance is another ideal which influenced our nation's founding. This has made our country the celebrated melting pot of the world. No other nation has as large a population of such diverse religious

---

[101]   http://dictionary.reference.com/browse/protestant--work--ethic

[102]   http://www.politifact.com/florida/statements/2012/jun/20/marco-rubio/marco-rubio-says-us-admits-1-million-immigrants-ye/

composition. Men and women of all backgrounds and faiths are free to live, work, pray, learn, and seamlessly integrate as they so choose — and we hope they do. However, with these freedoms lies the possibility that a specific practice or tenet of any religion may not integrate or be within cultural norms; as long as the practice is not unlawful or threatening to public safety we believe it has a right to be protected under American law. In other words, an individual's religious-based inclination diverging from public expectations should not warrant government-endorsed intolerance (e.g., the cake baker who declined servicing a same-sex marriage as it was contrary to his religious beliefs and was then court-ordered to provide services or be fined[103]). Beyond the technical breach of separation of church and state, from a practical standpoint we view government-forced "tolerance" which bureaucratically dictates who deserves "more" tolerance as not tolerant at all. Rather, genuine tolerance is a two-way street — the best way to ultimately reach all-inclusive tolerance (or at least as close as possible). This is how we expect religious liberty to play out.

Liberals also value the idea of separation of church and state and religious freedom, but past events have shown that they often interpret and apply these ideals very differently from us. Left-leaning supporters have been known to protest what we view as humble and unobtrusive religious historical symbols, for instance a sculpture of the Ten Commandments in public spaces.[104] They have also taken issue with public use of the phrase "Merry Christmas," viewing it as a politically incorrect

---

103   http://www.wsj.com/articles/court-rules-baker-cant-refuse-to-make-wedding-cake-for-gay-couple-1439506296

104   http://www.nbcnews.com/id/8375948/ns/us_news/t/split-rulings-ten-commandments-displays/

religious assumption, versus the ways we see it: either a secular wintertime greeting or an innocuous probability-weighted saying given that more than three-quarters of Americans identify as Christian.[105] If we lived in a predominantly Muslim country, we would not think twice if we were greeted with "Happy Ramadan." Nevertheless, some retailers have been known to ban the phrase during holiday season marketing to avoid offending sensitive non-Christians.[106] Such protest against saying "Merry Christmas" is a hypocritical shame: the First Amendment guarantees right/to protest *and* free speech. Fortunately, this hypersensitive trend is waning.[107]

While we are watchful of public religious symbolism (including Christian and otherwise) intruding onto unconstitutional or just obnoxious territory, we recognize the historical fact that our country was founded on basic Judeo-Christian principles. After all, our Declaration of Independence references "God" and our "Creator" (is it only a matter of time when someone claims to take offense over this?). So simultaneous to our belief in separation of church and state and support for religious freedom and diversity, we understand the natural predispositions for Judeo-Christian-based references in the U.S. Some everyday examples of this include currencies stamped with "In God We Trust" as well as public office closures on Sundays and often Saturdays based on a Judeo-Christian Sabbath (note the weekend in most Muslim nations takes place on Friday and Saturday based on the Muslim Sabbath). We generally view such unassuming religious-based aspects of

---

105   http://www.gallup.com/poll/159548/identify-christian.aspx
106   http://adage.com/article/news/christmas-winning-war-christmas/147195/#list
107   http://www.forbes.com/sites/pauljankowski/2011/12/15/is-saying-merry-christmas-politically-correct-good-for-business/

society as being of historical meaning or traditional gesture. And with credit to our Founding Fathers, we have the freedom to personally decide what such symbols and gestures mean to us (if anything at all) — historical, festive, religious, moral, artistic, or so on. While the Left is more inclined to feel offended by alleged encroachments on nonbelievers' religious liberties, we view any subtle presence not as something of religious indoctrination or superiority, but rather as part of our nation's origins — one which we hope all Americans can acknowledge or appreciate, if not celebrate.

Marijuana

Liberal Accusation: Opposing legalization of marijuana is a frivolous conservative attack on free will.

BHC Counter: While I do not believe that legalizing recreational marijuana is a constructive decision, I am in favor of legalization for medical purposes. Similar to many drugs which are beneficial under specifically prescribed conditions but subject to abuse and addictions otherwise, marijuana fits the bill. I believe that responding to the marijuana debate in all-or-nothing terms based on popularly-referenced personal anecdotes from college or unscientific comparisons with legal drugs (e.g., alcohol, tobacco) does not give this issue the serious, comprehensive consideration it deserves. Based on research finding troublesome effects of marijuana use, I anticipate health (e.g., mental instability), safety (e.g., DUI increases), and employment concerns (e.g., liabilities) to be just a few unintended consequences of an otherwise "harmless" drug.

As it stands now, four states (Alaska, Colorado, Oregon, and Washington) and D.C. permit marijuana purchase and use.[108] For better or worse, these jurisdictions will serve as testing grounds for the recreational marijuana culture. While conservatives generally believe legalized recreational marijuana is an unwise policy, we are open to seeing results coming from these jurisdictions in the near-term and long-term. Maybe we will change our position, but our expected best case scenario involves any positive results, like increased tax revenues, to be eclipsed by negative consequences. We anticipate such consequences to include increased abuse support programs and childhood marijuana prevention programs (which would essentially be funded by the aforementioned extra tax revenue).

For many recreational supporters, the case for legalization comes from a desire to do away with relatively petty marijuana-related arrests and prison sentences. Conservatives would agree that law enforcement and prison space should be used more efficiently (see Incarceration section). Lawmakers in some states have already begun to lessen marijuana-related penalties to fines. We see this as the right alternative to a total legalization of marijuana.

Recreational marijuana supporters also argue that stigmas tied to marijuana are dependent on our "narrow-minded" cultural perspective. They reference places which have smoke shops as prevalent as coffee shops, and sometimes they are one and the same. However, simply noting the culture and accepted behavior of another country should not necessarily make the case for its adoption in the U.S. If it did then we could all make a case against indecency laws (actually, some liberals do), as

---

108   http://www.usatoday.com/story/money/business/2015/08/18/24-7-wall-st-marijuana/31834875/

some countries are accustomed to nudity in public parks. This argument serves better to justify a predetermined opinion than to provide meaningful persuasive thought.

We have seen cigarettes abound and the Big Tobacco industry prosper in spite of public service announcements and warning labels noting addiction and health risks to smokers and secondhand inhalers. Conservatives anticipate similar dynamics to occur with a recreationally legal "Big Marijuana" industry. Many refer to the budding industry (pun intended) as "Big Tobacco 2.0,"[109] though recreational supporters differentiate marijuana from tobacco by emphasizing that nicotine, the drug of a tobacco cigarette, is absent in marijuana and therefore makes it safe. That fact is as weak as noting that nicotine is absent from cocaine — each is its own drug bringing its own consequences. Marijuana is no exception.

Scientific reports have documented the downside following the initial marijuana high. Regardless of how it gets into your system, it affects every organ in your body, the nervous system, and the immune system. A user is at higher risk of heart attack, lung-related health problems, paranoia, anxiety, depression, suicidal thoughts, and schizophrenia. Long-term users can have physical withdrawal symptoms like cravings, irritability, sleeplessness, and loss of appetite.[110] Responsible and occasional recreational users do not see these as realistic risks, using themselves as supportive "evidence." But unfortunately, not every recreational user is responsible, and "occasional" can

---

109   https://learnaboutsam.org/the-issues/big-tobacco-2-0-big-marijuana/
110   http://www.webmd.com/mental-health/addiction/marijuana-use-and-
       its-effects

be a very relative term. Understandably, recreational marijuana supporters highlight the argument that alcohol consumption carries its own set of risks (not so dissimilar from that of marijuana), yet is legal and commonplace. However, given the many considerations, we are not convinced at this time that it makes sense to have recreational use of marijuana legalized. Developments to come from the current five jurisdictions permitting recreational marijuana will shed more complete light on the effects of legalization. This will enable Americans to more thoroughly weigh the benefits against the consequences, including the exposed unintended consequences.

Science

Conservatives encourage appropriately incorporating new discoveries, scientific advancements, and general modernization in how we approach policy. In fact, the conservative principle of competition looks to advance the status quo of any institution or society (within a moral framework), and science plays a huge role in that. Contrary to what some liberals believe, conservatives are not anti-science religious zealots opposed to teaching evolution in science curricula. This allegation is as ridiculous as a claim that liberals support Ebonics in grammar curricula.[111] While an insignificant segment within a party may hold a wayward view, it is absolutely not a defining platform or mainstream perspective. Nevertheless, through headlining extreme and the plainly false information, media outlets have proven time and again to be effective purveyors of distortion from what mainstream conservatives actually

---

[111]   http://www.nbcnews.com/id/8628930/ns/msnbc-the_ed_show/t/
does-ebonics-belong-curriculum/#.Vj6w0rerT4Z

believe. The reality is that science and technology, specifically the discoveries made within those fields, are highly respected by conservatives. We rely on the individual human spirit and its abilities to invent and discover solutions for mankind — feats that government bureaucracies are far less capable of achieving. Accordingly, we reference science and technology in how we apply our philosophies.

Environment

Liberal Accusation: You do not care about the well-being of our planet.

BHC Counter: I actually care a great deal about our planet. I support ecofriendly initiatives like clean energy, recycling, and conservation efforts. After all, the importance of conserving, protecting, and not wasting is inherent in our name: "*Conserve*-atives." I am strongly opposed to wasting resources, from natural resources to fiscal resources. I care about wildlife, agriculture, and parks just the same as any right- or left-leaning person who recognizes we are all part of a complex ecosystem. At the same time, I support economic initiatives such as job creation and everyday expense reductions when they do not severely compromise nature.

An important environmental debate today is one which questions the point at which the goal of economic progress encroaches on the goal of environmental safety. We do not find these two goals to be mutually exclusive. Many liberals, though, continue to be outraged by some economically stimulating projects which they insist (often with their data, only to be countered by opposing data) come at the catastrophic expense to the environment. This same debate put another way questions when government environmental regulations excessively encroach upon individual freedoms (e.g., restrict certain job opportunities, increase personal spending due to government mandates).

Recent debate over fracking has been a prime example of how liberals falsely perceive environmental sacrifice in the spirit of greedy financial gain. To break this topic down (pun intended):

"Fracking" is shorthand for hydraulic "fracturing," in other words "breaking," which doesn't sound as strangely unpleasant. Fracking companies break through underground rocks with the help of physical and chemical elements to access oil and natural gas pockets. Fracking protesters unequivocally assert that the chemicals will contaminate underground water supply. If we saw validity in their absolute claims, we would not support fracking. However, even environmental organizations like the Environmental Protection Agency support fracking, stating that the process enables America's efforts for a clean energy future because natural gas pollutes less (i.e., reduces our carbon footprint) than traditional energy sources:

> Natural gas plays a key role in our nation's clean energy future. The U.S. has vast reserves of natural gas that are commercially viable as a result of advances in horizontal drilling and hydraulic fracturing technologies, enabling greater access to gas in shale formations. Responsible development of America's shale gas resources offers important economic, energy security, and environmental benefits.[112]

---

[112]   https://www.epa.gov/hydraulicfracturing

Fracking also enables economic opportunities, especially for the middle class. Middle-class unemployment and income growth have been of particular concern since the Great Recession of 2008, but fracking and fracking-related projects have created millions of jobs for this struggling socioeconomic class.[113] And these job opportunities could increase if anti-fracking politicians would ease regulatory hurdles. Ultimately, fracking translates to increased access to American energy — oil and, more significantly, natural gas. This boosts overall domestic energy supply, resulting in lower energy and gas prices for all Americans and serving as budgetary relief especially for the middle class. A related and equally favorable outcome is increased energy independence — freedom from dealing with some corrupt Middle East leaders who control much of the world's oil supply.

Global warming, also known as "climate change" (when "warming" is inconsistent with some of the brutal winters experienced over the past few years), is an issue which finds scientists arguing both sides of the debate. The liberal position claims that the earth is warming to critically high temperatures at an unusual rate. The conservative position claims that the earth's temperature fluctuation is a naturally continuous and cyclical phenomenon (e.g., from temperate to ice age and back). Scientists and environmental experts who find that temperature fluctuations are cyclical occurrences consider dire climate change claims to be unsubstantiated; however they do not receive the same media attention as those with an alarmist perspective. Professor Richard Lindzen of M.I.T. has come out in support of fellow scientists who were targets of recent liberal-generated witch hunts because they "question

---

113   http://www.bloomberg.com/news/articles/2012-10-23/fracking-will-support-1-7-million-jobs-study-shows

the popular alarm over allegedly man-made global warming."[114] He notes that those who do not adopt the mainstream view regarding global warming have been "relentlessly attacked... [and] the attacks have taken a threatening turn," jeopardizing the reputations and livelihoods of professors, scientists, and researchers who take a view opposite pop-politicized culture.

The ongoing debate illustrates how anyone with a preexisting agenda can find statistics supporting a particular position. As liberals see it, the planet experienced a rise in temperature which calls for urgency and government regulation to stop human-induced warming. On the other hand, conservatives find it noteworthy that this rise accounts for a literal fraction of a degree, and therefore we question allegations that temperature changes are something far more concerning than cyclical fluctuations. After weighing both sides and statistics of the debate, we view this global warming panic as excessive. That alone however, is not our concern. Consequently, the government's excessive regulatory burdens imposed on traditional energy sources are irrational. For example, one effect that is ignored or discounted by environmentalists is the increase in energy costs, which largely burden the lower and middle classes. This immediate consequence drastically outweighs any potential positive impact of what will only be incrementally less greenhouse gas emission.[115] The anticipated decrease in U.S. emissions accounts for only a small fraction of total global emissions — for every step we might take forward in clean energy, China, India, and other emerging economies take the world many steps back. This is not to say that we should

---

114   http://www.newsmax.com/US/climate-change-global-warming-MIT-Richard-Lindzen/2015/03/05/id/628562/

115   http://www.cato.org/blog/002degc-temperature-rise-averted-vital-number-missing-epas-numbers-fact-sheet

not try for clean energy — we should! However, this does have us question government's environmental regulatory imposition which offers more symbolism than a practical impact (Dennis Prager refers to this as "feeling good vs. doing good," which we find can frequently apply to liberal policy approaches[116]). As with nearly all matters, government overregulation inhibits the opportunity, mobility, and economic benefits that enable people to overcome environmental challenges.

The environmental issue illustrates just another reason why in most cases viable and effective solutions cannot be found with more federal regulation. Rather, we prefer to address these challenges with innovative solutions which will fundamentally (not bureaucratically) shift private individuals and businesses to efficient and clean energy sources. In the meantime, government needs to appropriately prioritize pressing matters at stake. We want the federal government to focus time and resources on solving crises with devastating real-time consequences (e.g., fighting ISIS) and improving situations — largely through deregulation — with critical near-term need (e.g., workforce participation at a pitiful 38-year low[117]).

Based on philosophies and policy approaches, we view conservatism as generally having more confidence in human determination and ability than its political counterpart, liberalism. Accordingly, we recognize that private innovation and market forces, not government interference and regulation, inspire sustainable solutions to many societal and global issues — this includes environmental matters.

---

[116]   http://www.nationalreview.com/article/361839/feeling-good-vs-doing-good-dennis-prager

[117]   http://www.usnews.com/news/the-report/articles/2015/07/16/unemployment-is-low-but-more-workers-are-leaving-the-workforce

For example, the 19th century Malthusian theory forecasted that looming overpopulation would lead to mass starvation. Fortunately, this prediction was thwarted with Dr. Norman Borlaug's invention of dwarf wheat. Dwarf wheat, a genetically modified organism (popularly known as "GMO"), made farming practices more efficient and enabled increased production — just some of the many innovations coming out of the "Green Revolution." Ironically, this revolution may sound like a left-wing environmental activist movement, but it actually refers to years of mid-19th century scientific research supporting innovations involving hybrid agricultural breeding, irrigation drilling, and chemical fertilization.

Dr. Borlaug is credited with saving more than a billion people from starvation through advanced agricultural production, which was especially needed in the developing world. Such innovative science-based techniques (which by the way are now condemned by anti-GMO, Monsanto-protesting environmentalists) also contributed to environmental preservation. These techniques improved the productivity of land already in agricultural production, thus saving millions of acres that would otherwise have been put into agricultural use.[118] Dr. Borlaug's work continues to feed citizens around the world, especially people living in third world countries. Similar to these challenges of the past, we are confident that today's global environmental challenges can be efficiently overcome with human innovations such as clean energy (e.g., fracked natural gas, solar, wind), as well as sources and solutions on the brink of discovery.

For a host of reasons, we believe liberals are irrationally panicked over today's environmental matters and in turn

---

[118] http://www.encyclopedia.com/topic/Green_Revolution.aspx

irrationally angered toward anyone who disagrees — those they perceive to be "anti-science, climate-change deniers."[119] But the discord itself is not our main concern. Rather, the core issues for conservatives are the negative consequences of liberal politicians' inefficient regulatory impositions, as well as the consequences of their failure to prioritize addressing more pressing matters. For example, we disagree with the current liberal White House administration's State of the Union declaration that climate change poses the greatest threat to future generations.[120] Instead we view today's increasingly deadly terrorist activities (e.g., ISIS committing genocide in the Middle East, executing terror plots worldwide, and strengthening its network to empower attacks on U.S. soil) to be tremendously greater threats to future generations, as well as present-day populations. So while we agree that we should all do good — very good — for the environment (e.g., recycle, reduce carbon emissions), we also believe that pop-political priorities have run askew. If government would redirect the vitality it puts into environmental issues toward the underwhelming effort they have made against horrifying current realities of terrorism, we all (at home and abroad) would be in a much safer and promising present-day circumstance — *this* would be the best foundation for future generations.

Stem Cell Research

Liberal Accusation: You oppose stem cell research because of your religious beliefs.

---

[119]   http://www.wsj.com/articles/the-unsettling-anti-science-certitude-on-global-warming-1438300982

[120]   http://thehill.com/policy/energy-environment/230146-obama-declares-climate-greatest-threat-to-future-generations

BHC Counter: I actually support scientific research and medical advancements, including those relating to stem cells. Any religious beliefs I may have are irrelevant to how I approach this issue. Stem cell research has led to amazing discoveries and innovations, ranging from academic insights to practical applied benefits. Along with fellow conservatives, I recognize that the discoveries made from such research have proven invaluable to humanity. A conservative platform, both from a religious and secular perspective, embraces advancements in the sciences just as it does in any other area where innovation can improve lives.[121]

Liberals wildly mistake our disapproval of certain stem cell-testing practices, specifically human embryonic testing (e.g., cloning, eugenics), as an all-encompassing opposition to stem cell research. This falsehood seems to align with other liberal tales, such as our alleged opposition to teaching human evolution in classrooms. The reality is that we support all efforts for scientific advancements *except* where there is disregard for the sanctity of innocent human life. In other words, a line is crossed when stem cell research involves meddling with or testing on an embryo (a fertilized egg which grows to a fetus which grows to a baby). Just as animal rights activists (typically of the liberal persuasion) find that animal testing crosses a moral line, we believe that embryo testing crosses a very serious moral line, but also a very significant practical line.

Beyond the morality of embryo-involved stem cell research, practical consequences must also be noted. Who are the people willing to give or sell their reproductive cells for scientific use? Will they serve as the parents if the embryo tests require coming

---

[121]   http://2012.republican-candidates.org/Romney/Stem-Cell.php

to term (i.e., the embryos survive to experience his or her birth)? Or will the scientifically created human engineered for research purposes (i.e., created for a purpose other than its own independent life) be owned by an institution or cared for by a parent? Controversial variations of stem cell testing also include procedures of human cloning as well as eugenics — the science of improving a human population by controlled breeding to increase the occurrence of desirable heritable characteristics.[122]

The fact is that conservatives support stem cell research. As with many closely held opinions, however, there are limitations; in this case, as long as research and testing do not compromise the inviolability of human life or generate unethical unintended consequences. Nevertheless, the issue has become a liberal propaganda point delivered by some who wish to sustain the grossly misleading characterization that conservatives are anti-science. The fact is that conservatives are not anti-science religious zealots standing in the way of medical progress. This far less sensational reality is that the overall stem cell debate is not a high priority political debate for conservatives but more importantly, we encourage such research for medical advancement.

---

[122] http://www.oxforddictionaries.com/us/definition/american_english/eugenics

PART IV
FOREIGN POLICY

Foreign Relations

Conservatives believe that forging strong, positive relationships with our international neighbors is a practical and moral obligation. We support relationships demonstrating cooperation and loyalty toward our allies, diplomacy toward potential allies, and boldness toward adversaries. Further, we want strong policies to reflect our vision of America's global leadership and for how the world recognizes American leadership contributions. A strategic foreign relations policy is critical in maintaining our role as the leader of the free world. Foreign relationships inevitably include social and fiscal elements. In step with this, the conservative principles we apply to domestic issues also apply to foreign issues. The following sections outline conservative views on foreign relations and how these matters fit into the bigger picture of retaining (and currently to some degree regaining) an effective and respected role in the world.

Leadership

Liberal Accusation: America's assumption of global leadership is arrogant.

BHC Counter: I believe our country's capabilities, moral fiber, and national interest drive us to take on a role as the world leader — a role which aims to protect and inspire good in the world. Given qualities of freedom, equality, democracy, sacrifice, virtue, and charity, I believe that the U.S. is most capable of this calling. Refusing to reliably respond would be immoral and unreasonable, as well as arguably xenophobic and selfish. Fortunately, a long history of our country rising to the occasion — utilizing our good will, diplomacy, resolve, and strength — has established our country's leadership reputation. Nevertheless, I realize that enduring as leader of the free world can be more challenging than working toward it, so I appreciate how conservatives do not approach our nation's leadership tasks lightly.

A conservative foreign leadership policy would be *unlike* that which we have seen over the past few years: we *would* stand by and work with our proven allies (as has not been the case with Israel); we would offer an olive branch to adversaries *only after* they have demonstrated positive change (as has not been the case with Cuba); we would *not* risk exploitation of premature dealings in hopes that adversaries will demonstrate cooperation (as has not been the case with Iran); and we would *not* assume adversarial governments are reasonable actors (as has not been the case with Russia). In addition to the significance of deciding on approaches and actions to take, the significant consequences of deciding on pacifist inaction can be just as grave (e.g., Syria). Certainly, in deciding any kind of policy action there is no such thing as "guaranteed" (e.g., Iraq War); however, as a leader, tough decisions on how to act must be made based on available intelligence information and staying true to American principles.

Our country's leadership position in large part comes from our unique ability to economically support and cooperate with nations of aligned interests, regardless of their own economic circumstance. If a nation faces obstacles which prevent its citizens from realizing prosperity and peace, the U.S. provides assistance. If potential synergies exist between us and another nation, the U.S. offers partnership. We are also in a position to exercise warnings through economic boycotts when countries are severely misaligned with our value system; for example, regarding human rights. Taking a stand is a leadership quality which conservatives are very willing to leverage.

U.S. military support for foreign allies, specifically calling for our men and women in uniform to risk their lives on foreign front lines, is a much more controversial matter. No one, conservative or liberal, wants our military at unnecessary risk over futile purposes. Many Democrats and Libertarian-Republicans go further, more staunchly believing our military and its resources should stay out of foreign conflicts. However, most conservatives view selective and strategic military support for our allies as not just a morally-essential leadership effort but also a national interest effort. Free nations look to the U.S. to act in solidarity, and oppressed citizens of authoritarian states look to us to deliver hope; at the same time, helping to defend the good by fighting the bad weakens the enemy and its potential to wage future attacks which may eventually be aimed directly at the U.S. (e.g., Nazis; see Military section).

Our significant role in the world, largely by virtue of the strong relationships forged with other nations, is not simply a matter of pride for conservatives. Rather, it is an understanding that a power vacuum would ensue without the U.S. acting and serving in a leadership role. More concerning, this power vacuum would be immediately filled by another major economic or geopolitical power player, but one with a government of questionable-to-corrupt values (e.g., Russia, China). In such a precarious situation, the real intentions of competing international players are unclear at best. Needless to say, we have much more confidence in the leadership intentions of our own country rather than the leadership intentions of alternative global powers.

Free Trade

Liberal Accusation: You support cheaper foreign workers and take jobs away from Americans.

BHC Counter: I support free trade, which ties into my overarching conservative principles of limited government and economic freedom. With free trade policy, countries are able to import and export as guided by supply and demand, under natural commercial competition, rather than as dictated by government influence (e.g., via import and export tax impositions). I do believe, however, that there are circumstances which call for appropriate government influence on free (and fair) trade. For example, I do not support commerce with corrupt governments of other nations (e.g., North Korea, Iran, Cuba) that violate basic moral principles. I find government-imposed economic sanctions to be a reasonable tool to seek moral compliance. Outside of these specific cases, I generally believe free trade policy is ideal for long-term productivity and prosperity. While I root for America to hold the best jobs in the global marketplace (after all, I believe my fiscal policy positions engender this), I do not believe that restricting free trade agreements is a prudent or effective means of making that happen.

Some may find our position on free trade counterintuitive, as conservatives tend to be labeled as nationalistic, using every opportunity to support "American-made" (a la our Ford pick-up trucks). While that does seem to be the case relative to our liberal counterparts, we actually view the idea of free trade as a very American practice, one involving competition and cooperation. This position assumes a level playing field where foreign currency manipulation is not used as a tool to corrupt trade balance, nor is the abuse of foreign workers used to inappropriately reduce the cost of production. If another country can equitably deliver a better good or service, more power to it. American ingenuity will respond by either creating a better product or service (see Capitalism section) or focusing on other deliverables more critical or more in demand.

Liberals tend to view free trade policies as American job killers. As demands for goods and services shift or as currency rates change in favor of foreign trade partners, a number of jobs will follow suit overseas. Conservatives are more inclined to see free trade as an efficient policy which creates incentives for improvements. Free trade keeps prices of goods and services lower for the American consumer. At the same time free trade incentivizes American businesses to continue to innovate in order to remain viable in the global marketplace. This in turn creates new and better jobs for American workers.

Free trade is essentially international capitalism (see Capitalism section). In line with capitalist dynamics, we value free trade for its commercial approach in making the world more cooperative and inspiring global economic progress. Globalization is today's reality, which ought to be embraced. Anything but a general free trade policy would artificially hold back worldwide progress. All participating nations, from the U.S. to developing countries, benefit from the positive effects (e.g., the "growing pie") of free trade.

Israel

Liberal Accusation: You blindly support Israel in spite of its occupation of and aggression toward Palestine.

BHC Counter: I support Israel primarily because I appreciate the country's political and economic practice of democracy and freedom, a value system very similar to our own. This is no different than the reasons we support many of our other allies. However, unlike our other allies, Israel withstands nearby neighbors who brazenly espouse hatred and violence toward the Jewish State. These neighboring countries hold anti-Semitic hostilities rooted in radicalized and historical religious bigotry. I believe the very real threats from places like Iran and Palestine require U.S. solidarity in response. My support for the peaceful existence of Israel and views on the Israeli-Palestinian dispute are distinct but related matters. The creation of Israel, though ethically and legally sound, came with much controversy stemming from adjacent Palestine and a few other Muslim neighbors. I believe that the criticism of Israel regarding its handling of Palestinian attacks and the general circumstances in the region is the result of narrow focus on propaganda favoring the Palestinian cause. But even as I consider the other claims, I find it difficult not to question the credibility of a state tainted by a governing body shaped by an internationally recognized terrorist organization (i.e., Hamas) and endorsed by an internationally recognized terror sponsor (i.e., Iran).[1]

Unlike the unnerving declarations of many of its neighbors, conservatives support Israel's right to exist in principle and in international law. The Jewish State of Israel was designated by the U.N. in 1948 to support displaced European Jews and holocaust survivors after World War II.[2] The area of land used to establish Israel was formerly a geopolitical entity under British administration (known as The British mandate). The U.N. resolution also concurrently established the Arab State of Palestine. Since the creation of Israel, Israeli leaders and citizens (including Jews, Christians, and Muslims) have acted as a nation of democracy and freedom, and as a loyal ally to the U.S. Unfortunately, Muslims living in the formerly British-owned region viewed and continue to view the formation of a Jewish State as an invasion of Jews onto Muslim holy land (note, however, they did not take similar issue when this land was under British control). The mere existence of Israel continues to produce hostility among some of its Muslim neighbors. These feelings are escalated by matters including the people's Jewish faith, its "Western" culture, its friendship with the U.S., and its unyielding efforts to defend its right to exist in peace.

It is no secret that certain countries, leaders, and organizations in the Middle East harbor anti-Semitic as well as anti-Western sentiment. Prominent notorious leaders in the Middle East

---

1   http://www.washingtoninstitute.org/policy-analysis/view/replacing-hamas-irans-new-proxy-militia-in-gaza
2   https://history.state.gov/milestones/1945-1952/creation-israel

(e.g., Iranian presidents and ayatollah supreme leaders) brazenly assert that Israel has no right to exist, declaring statements such as, "Israel is a wound on the body of the world of Islam that must be destroyed."[3] Words like these only scratch the surface of the rhetoric made by some of Israel's anti-Semitic neighbors. The same characters who boast anti-Israel sentiment also declare hatred for the West, especially the U.S.: "And God willing, with the force of God behind it, we shall soon experience a world without the United States and Zionism."[4] Our support for Israel is not simply a cliché case of "my enemy's enemy is my friend." Rather it is a reality in which a group openly wants to destroy anyone who represents a value system unlike its own — this happens to include Israeli Jews and Americans. The vitriol coming from anti-Israel countries only furthers our conviction that America must stand by our ally Israel in its ever-vigilant effort to defend itself against these instigators.

Unfortunately, the hate and threats are not limited to words. Attacks from Palestine have routinely come in the form of missile strikes and ground assaults — said to be in retaliation against Israeli occupation within Palestinian territory. Israel asserts that alleged areas of occupation are based on misleading Palestinian claims, and that Israel's efforts to secure its borders are no different than Egypt's *accepted* efforts to do so similarly around Palestine (a classic double standard).[5] Israel, on the other

3   https://www.washingtonpost.com/news/worldviews/wp/2013/08/02/iranian-presidents-comments-on-israel-are-latest-flashpoint-in-war-of-perceptions/
4   http://www.cnn.com/2005/WORLD/meast/10/26/ahmadinejad/
5   https://www.washingtonpost.com/news/worldviews/wp/2015/07/02/does-israel-actually-occupy-the-gaza-strip/

hand, claims that the areas where it maintains controversial presence are legally disputed territories and therefore Israeli presence (which they reiterate is *not* occupation) is justifiable.[6] Nevertheless, the U.N. has deemed Israel's settlements to be in violation of Palestinian human rights. It is worth mentioning here that for some time now, many (conservatives, in particular) have come to view today's United Nations as a controversial, self-serving, self-righteous, hypocritical, bureaucratic entity for a host of reasons unrelated to the Israeli-Palestinian conflict (e.g., moral relativism in the face of genocide and terrorism, kickbacks, and bribes among U.N. officials).[7][8][9] So we keep this in mind when taking U.N. judgments into consideration. Its attention on Israel's treatment of Palestine has shown to be excessive, with "a third of all critical resolutions passed by [the U.N.] Human Rights Commission during the past forty years directed exclusively at Israel. By way of comparison, there has not been a single resolution even mentioning the massive violations of human rights in China, Russia, North Korea, Cuba, Saudi Arabia, Syria, or Zimbabwe."[10] Even U.N. Secretary-General Ban Ki-Moon admitted that the U.N. has shown bias against Israel.[11]

United Nations aside, while decades-long modern day battles and centuries-old religious wars very much distort the original

---

6   http://mfa.gov.il/MFA/ForeignPolicy/FAQ/Pages/FAQ_Peace_process_
     with_Palestinians_Dec_2009.aspx#Settlements1

7   http://www.humanrightsvoices.org/site/commentary/?p=208

8   http://blogs.aljazeera.com/blog/americas/un-ordered-compensate-
     whistleblower

9   http://www.economist.com/node/4267109

10   A Lethal Obsession: Anti-Semitism from Antiquity to the Global Jihad,
     Robert Wistrich, p. 487, January 2010

11   http://www.ynetnews.com/articles/0,7340,L-4418776,00.html

catalyst or a perspective of right versus wrong, it is indisputable that today's Palestinian ruling organization, known as Hamas, sponsored by Iran (hardly a promising affiliation), prioritizes the destruction of Israel and Jews over regional peace or its own internal peace. With Hamas' practice of sending suicide bombers into Israel and using actively operating Palestinian schools and hospitals as rocket launch sites and militant shelters, its barbaric tactics should not go unnoticed.[12][13] Hamas is designated as a terrorist organization not only by Israel, but also the U.S., Egypt, and many other nations worldwide.[14] In early 2015 the Palestinian Authority and the Palestinian Liberation Organization were found guilty in a Manhattan court of their role in supporting six terrorist acts in Israel between 2002 and 2004, which killed and injured Israelis and Americans. We view these facts as reflections of Palestinian leaders' egregious attitudes and objectives. With this, our instincts are only confirmed — it is in our moral and national interest to stand with our ally, Israel.

In spite of Israel's history as a nation of democracy and freedom, and regardless of the attacks Israel has endured by enemies who are on America's terror list, many liberals are inclined to wholly smear and write off Israel's standing given the Palestinian claim of Israeli occupation and aggression. At best a liberal stance is an impartial one, so as to not offend either of the conflicting sides. Conservatives, on the other hand, are committed to the support of Israel — not blindly, but rather conscientiously. Israel is our longest-standing ally in the Middle

---

12   http://news.bbc.co.uk/2/hi/middle_east/3256858.stm

13   http://www.washingtonpost.com/news/morning-mix/wp/2014/07/31/
      why-hamas-stores-its-weapons-inside-hospitals-mosques-and-
      schools/

14   http://www.bbc.com/news/world-middle-east-31674458

East and one of our most demonstrated allies in the world. Its volatile regional circumstances fueled by Islamic extremist terrorist organizations (e.g., Hamas in Palestine, Hezbollah in Lebanon) are not threats that Israelis should face without our backing.

Middle East

Liberal Accusation: Your approach to Middle East affairs elicits more instability and corruption.

BHC Counter: My approach regarding Middle East affairs always favors positive, diplomatic relationships, just as it does with any region in the world. Fortunately, the fact is that many of our relationships with Middle East/Muslim countries are currently characterized by positive associations (e.g., Jordan, Egypt, Afghanistan, Turkey). However, a sweeping generalization one way or another could not accurately describe our situation with the region given its complexities — our relationships with each country are as distinct as fingerprints on the same hand. In contrast to those countries with which we foster healthy and productive partnerships, leadership of other countries (e.g., Iran, Syria) have crossed lines away from morality and civility, making diplomatic efforts terribly inadequate — or rather futile. I believe the U.S. approach to relations with countries demonstrating irrational, unethical, and violent behaviors requires austerity and strength. Sanctions and at times military flexing may appropriately achieve the goal of stability for the overall region, most directly benefitting our Middle East allies, and ultimately our national security.

Middle East turmoil is largely motivated by internal extremist Islamic entities tainting an entire region. It is not simply a matter of Muslim versus non-Muslim or harboring resentment towards the U.S.; rather, the conflicts involve dynamics much more internally complex (e.g., Sunnis versus Shiites, moderates versus radicals). As King Abdullah of Jordan declared, "Confronting extremism is both a regional and international responsibility, but it is mainly our battle, us Muslims, against those who seek to hijack our societies and generations with intolerant takfiri ideology."[15] Takfiri refers to the radical Islamic practice of declaring nonbelievers worthy of death. As King Abdullah put it, a drop of venom can poison a well.[16]

The region's turmoil is largely sustained and exacerbated by wealth amassed from the region's oil supply. The Middle East sits atop almost one-third of the world's oil production[17] and as a result controls a meaningful portion of the world's oil resources. The money generated from oil production is paid to the leaders sitting on these oil fields (e.g., Saudi Arabia, Iraq, Iran, UAE). Consequently, corrupt leaders from some of these nations use oil money to fund terrorist organizations. The power and sustainability of groups like Al Qaeda and ISIS (Islamic State of Iraq and Syria) are fueled by money generated from Middle East oil. Relating the matter to domestic politics, this foreign control of oil further supports the case for U.S. energy independence, which is achieved through technologies such as fracking (see Environment section). The approach towards stability in the Middle East — and effectively U.S. relationships

---

15   http://www.timesofisrael.com/jordan-king-urges-muslims-to-lead-fight-against-terror/

16   http://www.breitbart.com/national-security/2015/09/28/king-jordan-un-struggle-outlaws-islam-third-world-war/

17   http://www.eia.gov/beta/international/rankings/#?prodact=53-1&cy=2014

with the region's nations — would become less complex if our government would allow energy independence capabilities to free our country from Middle East oil dependency. This would significantly curb the funding of and hence weaken the power of Middle East-based terror groups.

Conservatives look to recognize and seize upon opportunities for goodwill and peace within the Middle East. Though some liberals may allege that we have a greedy ulterior motive to control the region's oil, the truth is we actually much prefer energy self-sufficiency at home and peace in the Middle East — two very complementary goals. In addition to establishing allies, we find it equally important to recognize and call out areas of threat to peace and goodwill. Generally speaking, in any plan, identifying opportunities is as critical as identifying obstacles in order to achieve a goal. With regard to the region's significant obstacles, Iran is a clear threat. Since the Ayatollah's return to power in the late 1970s, Iran's newly extremist Islamic government has been vocal in its threats and hate towards the U.S. (e.g., "Death to America," "America is the Great Satan"[18]). The country's intention to obtain nuclear weapon capabilities has been widely recognized by many international players, from which U.S. sanctions and UN resolutions were based — then, not surprisingly, violated by Iran multiple times. Iran is a leading sponsor of terrorist organizations. It provides funding, equipment, weapons, training, and sanctuaries to the likes of Al Qaeda, the Taliban, Hezbollah in Lebanon, and Hamas in Palestine.[19] We cannot respect a regime demonstrating such behavior much less expect it to honor its diplomatic

---

18   http://www.wsj.com/articles/the-u-s-is-still-irans-great-
      satan-1437170607
19   http://www.cfr.org/iran/state-sponsors-iran/p9362

agreements. We certainly have little faith that Iran will uphold its end of the recently passed nuclear deal.

ISIS is a relatively newer threat but of greater, more imminent danger to regional and international stability. Considered a more radical offshoot of Al-Qaeda (which, by the way, continues to have a stronghold in other parts of the region), ISIS has come to prioritize domination of Iraq and Syria while also setting sights internationally for what they declare is in the name of a worldwide Islamic caliphate. With the threat of ISIS on their doorstep, our Middle East allies stepped up their military forces accordingly. The current liberal White House administration has yet to do so. We do not understand how the Left expects the horrific practices of ISIS (e.g., genocide, rape, sex slavery, burning, beheading) to be quelled by non-military to minimal-military effort. We believe it is critical to demonstrate timely and adequate solidarity via military partnership, not only for the support of our allies but ultimately for the sake of our national interests (ahead of the arrival of ISIS at our own doorstep). The terror of ISIS has already been experienced on American soil to a limited degree. With ISIS already having taken responsibility for one-off attacks within Europe and the U.S., halfhearted military involvement will not stop the momentum of evil making its way around the world. We see frightening parallels between the objectives of ISIS terrorists of today and the Nazi terrorists during WWII. Therefore, we want to see a similarly strong response with regard to how the U.S. handled a *nationalistic* ideological world threat (i.e., Nazis) and how the U.S. ought to be handling a *religious* ideological world threat (i.e., ISIS). Because ISIS is a different type of organization than were the Nazis, we understand that an identical military response could not be employed. Rather, similar response in terms of commitment and determination is necessary, leveraging modernized tactics, intelligence, and combat strategy, in order to defeat ISIS.

As a result of the difficult lessons learned from U.S. involvement in the Iraq war, American leaders have become far more reluctant to use our military ground forces on foreign lands. Placing our military men and women in harm's way continues to be an absolute last alternative. That said, inappropriately resisting military utilization also has the potential of bearing unfavorable consequences. We believe the U.S. can and should be doing more to lead the effort to destroy terrorism originating in the Middle East. We value military strength not just for the sake of its ability to destroy an enemy, but also for the goal of deterrence and setting the stage for stability. Therefore, we want to see the U.S. demonstrate solidarity (beyond rhetoric) with our Middle East allies, as we all look forward to a time when the region can be free from terror. Once stability and peace win over the region and in turn the world, Muslims, Christians, Jews, and other Middle Easterners will be able to truly thrive — culturally, socially, and economically.

National Defense

Conservatives view our national security as an overarching matter which arguably overrides all of the domestic fiscal and social issues debated within our borders. Without the confidence in and reality of our personal safety, a derivative of our national security, the rights and wrongs of *any* of these other policy matters discussed become moot points. National security is a policy area where conservatives believe government should take on its most active role. This issue alone has caused much debate in the political arena, particularly in the modern day, given exponential growth in technology capabilities and increasing terror threats, but more generally starting in the earlier days of our nation's founding. As noted by the National Constitution Center, "Since the beginning of our nation, we have grappled with how to 'provide for the common defense' and to protect the people and the nation from foreign and domestic threats — without compromising the civil liberties of citizens."[20]

Security

Liberal Accusation: Your hawkish stance on handling national security represents un-American acts of rights violations.

BHC Counter: Opinions related to our country's optimal national security strategy may be debatable, but I trust we can all agree that there are extreme and imminent dangers constantly threatening the U.S. I believe that the primary goal of national security is to maintain the safety of the nation's citizens. Accordingly, I recognize that our government's strategies to protect the nation's security must be at least a step ahead of these extreme threats (that is, proactive versus reactive). When policies fall short of this, threats become tragic realities (as we have witnessed with increasing frequency). Our laws should serve as the framework we use to build our national security programs but success must remain the ultimate goal. I believe that if we can agree on the objective, we can constructively discuss the much more complicated topic of implementation.

---

[20]   http://archive-org.com/page/752651/2012-11-25/http://
      constitutioncenter.org/constitution/issues/national-security

It is relevant to note that an overarching disconnect exists between conservative ideology and that of the current liberal White House administration with regard to the most serious threats facing national security. In the 2014 State of the Union address, the president declared that the greatest threat to national security is global warming (see Environment section).[21] This indicates a serious divergence from conservative priorities and perception. As national security relates to the conservative perspective, we see far more alarming threats that exist, such as ISIS, Russian aggression, and Iranian nuclear development. In comparison, we currently place global warming notably lower on the list of policy priorities.

One of the reasons a succinct and tidy policy is impossible is that the scope of national security is sprawling and touches on many other aspects of public policy (see Immigration, Surveillance, Military sections). National security measures (and consequently criticisms) cover a range of areas given the degrees and complexities of how malicious people can find ways to devastate safe environments. We realize that the U.S. is confronted with a vast and unrelenting array of global threats against our freedoms and lives (e.g., drug traffickers, cyber-hackers, terrorist massacres, and so on). For this reason, our country needs to be continually vigilant and virtually clairvoyant. The Department of Homeland Security (e.g., U.S. Border Patrol), the National Security Agency (e.g., metadata surveillance collection), and the USA Patriot Act (i.e., post-9/11 terrorism interception law) are several examples of government programs which have served as our nation's "eyes and ears" to prevent the staging and execution of major attacks. In spite

---

[21]   http://www.usnews.com/news/articles/2015/01/20/obama-no-greater-threat-than-climate-change

of earnest efforts *and many successes* in keeping all Americans safe, these policies have long been under criticism, notably for rights abuses. Allegations span from newer issues of IT security abusing privacy rights (e.g., Edward Snowden, Apple versus FBI) to long-established processes like the immigration system discriminating against foreigners. With regard to the more severe aspect of national security protection, offshore military prisons are often uncompromisingly criticized by the Left for human rights violations. We understand the moral dilemma at hand.

The argument we hear most commonly from liberals regarding rights violations in the name of national security is that "the ends don't justify the means." This is often referenced in the context of terrorist interrogation tactics at institutions such as Guantanamo Bay. It is also commonly concluded with the following rhetorical question: If we debase ourselves by employing the methods of our enemies, are we any better than our enemies? Our response would be that the question posed is not rhetorical, but rather ethical. Maintaining moral high ground may allow our government to look our enemy in the eye with a clear conscience, but that can come at the cost of being unable to face the citizens it has failed to protect (at the funerals of loved ones).

The facets of this debate are touched upon in a popular moral reasoning course at Harvard taught by Professor Michael Sandel and aptly titled *Justice*. He begins the first lecture by introducing a moral thought exercise:

Suppose you're the driver of a trolley car and your trolley car is hurtling down the track at 60 miles per hour. At the end of the track you notice five workers working on the track. You try to stop but you can't; your brakes don't work. You feel desperate because you know that if you crash into these five workers, they will all die. Let's assume you know that for sure. And so you feel helpless until you notice that there is, off to the right, a side track. And at the end of that track, there is one worker working on the track. Your steering wheel works so you can turn the trolley car, if you want to, onto the side track; killing the one but sparing the five. Here's our first question. What's the right thing to do?[22]

The remainder of the lecture goes through why the principle of "killing one to save five" is a moral ambiguity with no easy answer. However, when it comes to military prisons, and the incarceration and interrogation methods employed, we believe the moral dilemma becomes relatively less difficult. Our theoretical trolley car has been replaced with an actual terrorist threat. On its current course, this "trolley car" is on track to injure and kill hundreds of innocent people. "Turning the steering wheel onto the side track" has been replaced with measures taken toward enhanced interrogation of a terrorist affiliate: instead of "killing one," as in the professor's scenario, the cost becomes controversial handling of rights. In such a case, conservatism believes "steering onto the side track" is the preferred route.

Two rebuttals predictably follow: 1) What if the detainee is innocent? and 2) Doesn't that leave the military prison susceptible to becoming a bastion of abused power (e.g., Abu Ghraib)? With regard to the first rebuttal, it is actually in the interest of the U.S. to apprehend only acknowledged terror affiliates. It is our responsibility to ensure that we are not

---

utilizing time and resources focused on a person irrelevant to national security threats, and moreover, definitely not detaining innocent bystanders. In these situations, we must rely on the methodically trained judgment of those men and women we entrust to protect us from evil. In a perfect world, every detainee would be proven guilty beyond a reasonable doubt; but in this evidently imperfect world, sometimes we have to make the call that if it walks like a duck, quacks like a duck, and swims like a duck... it's probably a duck. That said we understand entrusting our government with this level of judgment is what gives the second rebuttal its weight.

We acknowledge that abuse of power can hold and has held true with government/military personnel violating both legal and moral conduct in these facilities. In such instances, we want to penalize the violators and hold them accountable for abusing their authority. And more broadly, we want to employ alternatively effective tactics for handling terrorist prisoners rather than, as liberals typically prefer, to scrap the institution altogether (as in the case of Guantanamo Bay). The disinterest in finding compromise is unreasonable on many levels. Upon a shutdown, displaced terrorist detainees would be reassigned to civilian maximum-security prisons on the continental U.S. These terrorists would be in closer proximity to everyday civilian life,[23] [24] putting Americans at increased risk (provoking a classic "Not in My Back Yard" dilemma), and in more intimate proximity to civilian American prisoners (a sensible breeding ground for terrorist recruitment). And if the prisoners are simply released, a portion of them (National Intelligence reports

---

23   http://usatoday30.usatoday.com/news/nation/2009-12-15-illinois-
      prison-terrorists_N.htm
24   http://www.denverpost.com/news/ci_28912665/u-s-officials-
      consider-colorados-supermax-terrorism-detainees

indicate between one-quarter and one-third) will reappear on the battlefield to return to terrorism, reengaging with the mission to kill Americans and others.[25] We prefer to have compromised reform which would blend political perspectives on the handling of captured terrorists without affecting the critical purposes served by these military prison facilities. Like many other issues, we look to weigh all the possible outcomes — good and bad, intended and unintended — when forming an opinion on policy.

Some of the military-style tactics applied to captured terrorists are without a doubt daunting. However, we acknowledge evidence that the use of enhanced interrogation techniques on dangerous, well-connected terrorists can elicit positive outcomes.[26] Specifically, surrendered intelligence may ultimately be used to save innocent lives from future attacks. Playing nice or "fair" (as per the subjective liberal arbiters of what constitutes fair) is not going to elicit information which can be used to help stop terror activity. There is no sense in keeping well-connected terrorists comfortable when they hold potential information on literal life-or-death plots. Nevertheless, we understand that the system in place may not be perfect and that we can always look to improve on tactics used to effectively handle terrorist prisoners.

Interestingly, the desire to improve the efficacy of national security initiatives is not as fervently voiced as is the desire to shut down various national security initiatives. We'll optimistically

---

25   http://www.npr.org/sections/thetwo-way/2012/09/06/160678301/
percent-of-detainees-who-return-to-terrorism-after-release-edges-
up

26   http://www.washingtonpost.com/wp-dyn/content/article/2009/04/20/
AR2009042002818.html

take this to mean that our government's national security operations are generally quite effective. We'll also take this to mean that national security critics remain safe from security threats and terrorist attacks, enabling them to voice their grievances with an immeasurably successful national security program. As we see it, maintaining assurances in our national security is one area in which citizens and our government should never become complacent or, for that matter, should never weaken. It is impossible to prove a negative (i.e., an attack that never happened) and the achievement of security does not make for a sensational media headline. Therefore successful national security efforts most often go unrecognized — unless they are criticized for controversy. We believe protesters of our national security operation generally take effective measures for granted.

National security is a fundamental tenet within conservatism. Relating this to our emphasis on *limited* government, conservatives believe national security is an area within the government's limited scope which must be federally overseen. Consequently, national security policy is a reflection of who we are as Americans, so we are able to understand (though not agree with) the reason liberals believe many of our national security measures to be un-American. In our view, however, we are unfortunately dealing with unique terrorist enemies who do not share American views on civil liberties, do not follow accepted rules of engagement, nor respect Natural Law (e.g., suicide bombers dismiss the natural human instinct of self-preservation). Therefore, national security measures must be approached differently from that which a more rational scenario would call for. These measures may not make liberals happy, but we understand that when life is at risk and liberty is in jeopardy, the pursuit of happiness becomes frivolous in the absence of our two most basic rights.

Surveillance

Liberal Accusation: So... where do you stand??

BHC Counter: The confusion on this issue exists because conservatives are known to hold either a hardline constitutional/libertarian perspective or a security-prioritizing/conservative perspective (liberals also demonstrate a similar dichotomy of opinions). With constitutional matters in mind, but not from a libertarian approach, I lean towards the latter: I support a *degree* of government surveillance in today's increasingly threatened environment because I want to protect all of my other constitutional rights and basic freedoms. I believe some privacy must be sacrificed *to an extent* if we seek the best chance for defense against dangers (e.g., terrorism) which threaten these very rights and freedoms. I recognize that defining concepts like "degree" and "extent" is critical in the surveillance debate, and will need to be fluid as we learn about new means of how enemies are capable of plotting and communicating. Generally speaking, opinions on the surveillance issue are largely bipartisan, as most would agree that a working balance must be struck between ensuring security and protecting privacy.

Although the Constitution contains no express right to privacy, several amendments refer to various aspects of privacy guaranteed to American citizens. Americans have come to expect a right to privacy, and fight for it when they feel their privacy is threatened. But privacy, as with most other legal concepts, is accepted and upheld in a manner of degree. It is expected that the daily behavior of American citizens should proceed largely free of government "eyes and ears." However, there are several everyday examples of blatant surveillance already in place. Many U.S. cities have surveillance cameras mounted in various inconspicuous areas to monitor and record the activity of people and their behavior. These cameras were invaluable in identifying the 2013 Boston bombers and helping bring them to justice. There are also traffic light cameras in at-risk intersections. These cameras cannot guarantee drivers obey the law but can assist in punishing those who do not. Of course the intent is also to incentivize law-abiding behavior — if a driver expects that he or she will be caught and punished for breaking a law then ensuing behavior will be more likely to observe the law. So Americans have already come to knowingly and subconsciously expect some degree of government surveillance.

As the surveillance issue steps into a more private realm, particularly involving cell phone and cyber activity, the debate becomes more controversial. Still, we recognize the need for such security-minded surveillance given the unfortunate reality that there are evil people in the world with increasingly intelligent and calculated ways to communicate plans to attack innocent people. As a result, the nature of terror plots (in frequency and severity) has dictated the extent to which surveillance and intelligence collection ought to take place. In 2001, then-President Bush signed the USA Patriot Act into law just after September 11th. This law was designed to enhance the speed, pervasiveness, and thoroughness with which the government could monitor communications in an effort to prevent future terrorist attacks. In 2011 President Obama signed the Patriot Sunsets extension act, which extended key provisions of the original USA Patriot Act. Congress has since further extended the act, with certain exclusions, through 2019.

In spite of bipartisan political support, some remain cynical of government's right to grant itself the ability to monitor its citizenry. The flurry of legal challenges catalyzed by Edward Snowden[27] largely contributed to the 2015 expiration of the authorization for the National Security Agency (NSA) to collect metadata on phone calls. Those who vehemently oppose federal monitoring tactics deem government surveillance an un-American slippery slope of rights infringement (e.g., Apple versus FBI). They believe that the government will abuse personal information gleaned from citizens' data collections — to their point, the IRS' misconduct involving unjustifiable audits of conservative political groups only served to reinforce this distrust. First, instances of government abuses should be strictly addressed and penalized accordingly; but second, our distrust of terrorists and traffickers vastly outweighs our distrust of the U.S. government. While conservatives will always stand by the importance of a *limited* government, especially one kept in-check by the people, we understand that government ought to play a critical role in certain areas — this is one such area.

From street cameras to communication metadata (i.e., summaries of data), we accept and appreciate these surveillance methods as a means of collecting relevant intelligence to make our country safer. Similar to how we view the practice of profiling (see Profiling section), we believe surveillance for the purpose of near- and longer-term security for the greater good justifies small personal sacrifice. Until there is a less intrusive

---

27   http://www.ibtimes.com/what-metadata-nsa-loses-surveillance-power-american-phone-calls-data-about-data-1947196

but comparably effective method of preventing terrorist and criminal activity, we support the reasonable degree and intention of surveillance as we know it today.

Military

Liberal Accusation: Your militant attitudes put American military lives at risk and stigmatize America with a warmongering reputation.

BHC Counter: I believe our men and women in uniform are among our country's most precious assets. A top national priority should be to honor, support, and protect our military personnel. They are a fundamental component of what makes our military strong and in turn our nation secure. Military strength, not necessarily through the act of force but first through the acts of preparation and readiness, helps to ensure the American way of life is not vulnerable to attack — an idea commonly referred to as "peace through strength." U.S. military support is also relied upon by foreign allies to assist in the event of an attack. That said I believe we absolutely must be much more selective in when and how our military should be employed.

Conservatives' belief in peace through strength sums up our attitude on military-related matters. We want to be prepared, ready, and willing to utilize our strong military, and we want the world to know. Adversaries should reconsider aggressive decisions and allies should know we can offer support. This serves as a first line of defense which avoids putting our military in harm's way. However, if and when evil chooses to attack peace, stability, and innocent lives, our military must be ready to counter. At this tipping point, American peace through strength switches gears to American strength begets peace.

Even in times of escalating conflict, conservatives prefer diplomatic action over military action to the extent possible. However, we understand that diplomacy can be only as effective as the other party's intentions — that is, only among adversaries honestly willing to compromise for the ultimate shared goal of peace. Unfortunately, not all countries' regimes (and absolutely no terrorist organizations) are well-intentioned. Therefore, we recognize the unfortunate reality that military response is at times necessary. More importantly, a *timely* response — neither hasty nor hesitant — is critical to ensure U.S. military efforts are employed most safely and efficiently. A timely, patient response avoids premature and unnecessary risk; nevertheless, a timely, expeditious response prevents the enemy from gaining momentum (e.g., taking more innocent lives, taking more territory, enlisting more recruits), which would create increasingly dangerous circumstances for our military. We view combative enemies like a virus: the longer the virus is able to grow without intervention, the disease becomes stronger, tougher to defeat, and ultimately fatal. Conservatives realize the unfortunate reality that such viral enemies (e.g., ISIS, Nazis) respond to the fear of a strong military — not the olive branches of diplomacy.

Nevertheless, liberals do not hesitate to criticize our confidence in a strong military, often highlighting only negatives and ignoring its values. They generally view U.S. military action as catalyzing more violence and anti-American sentiment. Conservatives believe that our military's overwhelmingly bold efforts to stop the advancement of threats and protect innocent lives should not be altogether rebuked by politicized anti-war sentiments emphasizing past mistakes. Rather, we recognize missteps, as in Iraq, so they are not repeated as the U.S. military continues to protect and defend.

Conservatives view federal funding of the Department of Defense among a top budget priority. Defense spending is much more than just building the biggest and best weapons to destroy the enemy. We want sufficient defense spending to provide our military with the best possible support, from combat equipment, to health care (e.g., a VA that works), to civilian transition. While liberals draw more awareness to allocating taxpayer money to traditional social entitlement issues, we want to draw more awareness to funding the ultimate entitlement: national security protected by brave fellow citizens in uniform.

The bottom line is, contrary to the accusations of warmongering, conservatives despise war and we do not want to put our military men and women in jeopardy. We want diplomacy to peacefully and efficiently reach an ultimate goal of stability — but we do not mistake diplomacy as being the end goal. When diplomacy proves ineffective with irrational leaders who inhibit progress toward the goal, we view adequately prepared military strength as an essential component to encourage peace and, if necessary, ultimately enforce peace. We understand that anti-war sentiment should be held close to all hearts; however, we hold defending good against evil even closer to our hearts.

PART V
POP-POLITICS

The politics of popular culture has become an institution. Those who set the tone of pop culture, from Hollywood celebrities to news media anchors to social media savants, have been successful at establishing a standard for socially acceptable politics and political candidate support. Unfortunately, conservatives and our beliefs are largely excluded from this pop-political cultural standard (i.e., the cool kids' table). For example, the hateful backlash actress Stacey Dash received for tweeting her support of then-candidate Mitt Romney versus the acceptance of her *Clueless* co-star actress Alicia Silverstone's support of Barack Obama. As a black conservative, the disapproval Dash received from the Left was even more hateful.[1] With the blessings and support of pop culture, liberals have come to self-righteously identify as the party of open minds and understanding, with compassion an obvious given. It seems that they can do or say no wrong in the court of pop-cultural opinion. Many on the Left are pardoned for some very

---

1   https://www.washingtonpost.com/blogs/therootdc/post/stacey-
dash-supports-mitt-romney-gets-racial-backlash-on-twitter-not-all-
blacks-must-be-democrats/2012/10/09/22f792b6-1229-11e2-be82-
c3411b7680a9_blog.html

uncompassionate practices — and actually cheered if they are directed at slamming the Right.

In the spirit of conservatism, calling out the pop-political culture challenges we face is by no means a proverbial pull of the victim card — that would be against our philosophy. Rather, it is simply recognizing the tools of the "competition." For instance, liberal-generated character assaults following a predictable tactic of spotlighting anything from a Republican's trivial gaffe to an extremist right-wing personality. From here, they design their distortion of conservatives: hard-hearted, warmongering bigots in the pocket of big money, or with big money in their pockets. It is demoralizing when a significant portion of society, particularly a peer group, has bought into this. But acknowledgment is a first step to overcoming challenges posed by having a political opinion condemned (and gravely misrepresented) by pop-politics. Beyond the "PR" challenges faced by conservative politicians, pop-politicized culture also affects ordinary, mainstream conservatives. "Closet conservatives" avoid revealing our right-leaning views, realizing the prejudices which come with thinking against the haloed liberal grain.

Media Partialities

Media, in a variety of forms, is a powerful means of mass communication to convey facts, opinions, entertainment, and ideas. The power of media can be used to inform, intrigue, entertain, and inspire. That power becomes stronger when these capabilities combine in a way which fundamentally influences its audience. With multifaceted capabilities, media can come in the form of news, entertainment, and academia.

Media bias becomes evident when communication of fact, opinion, entertainment, and ideas blur to favor its messenger's overt or subliminal personal message. Conservatives' issue with mainstream media bias is not simply a trite complaint made by right-wing Fox-watching audiences. Just as a liberal audience is rightfully displeased by the reporting style of Fox News, a conservative audience is rightfully displeased by the reporting style of many other major media outlets (e.g., *The New York Times, The Huffington Post*, MSNBC, to name a few). Of course, mainstream media is not necessarily so staunchly dichotomous, but the point is that contrary to what a non-conservative audience may assume, Fox News' right-leaning posture does not imply that the mainstream posture is therefore neutral. We view the mainstream media stance as left-leaning, and for liberals to suggest otherwise is disingenuous — it is inherent that they would perceive left-leaning perspectives as accurate.

With regard to news media, biases most obviously come in the form of headline word choice, anchor delivery, and contributors' political persuasion, but they also less obviously come in the form of story selection. News stories of the day are selected not by an unbiased algorithm, but by an editor. When an editor decides which news is worthy for airtime and which is not, traditionally he or she has a responsibility to resist falling into a trap of qualifying that decision based on personal opinions. Alas, news media bias, once intended to run against the integrity of journalism and reporting, is now almost inevitable. Media is, after all, big business in which profitability or corporate politics sometimes flies in the face of objectivity. Media bias now serves as a way for an audience to choose its go-to news source. Since journalistic and reporter neutrality were largely abandoned some time ago, and C-SPAN is not exactly as entertaining as left-loving/right-heckling programs like *The*

Daily Show, we are left with media run by executives, editors, and reporters who naturally have an agenda (as most do) and can subtly or not-so-subtly advance that agenda accordingly.

It is not surprising news to us that cable networks (e.g., CNN, MSNBC) donated more than $1 million to the Democratic Party versus less than $150,000 to the Republican Party in 2008.[2] But even in spite of media's strong skew towards making Democratic donations[3] and at times liberal self-admissions,[4] Democrats continue to brush off liberal media bias as a mere right-wing myth. A 2005 UCLA study looked to quantify the political bias of news media through a unique, standardized method comparing the messaging of various major outlets to the messaging of congressional lawmakers across the political spectrum. The study quantifiably and significantly concluded that media bias is real and "almost all major media outlets tilt to the Left."[5] Tim Groseclose, a UCLA political scientist and the study's lead author, noted that he "suspected that many media outlets would tilt to the Left because surveys have shown that reporters tend to vote more Democrat than Republican... But [he] was surprised at just how pronounced the distinctions are." The study analyzed news reporting (not opinion pieces) of 20 major media outlets, including *The New York Times*, *Los Angeles Times*, *The Wall Street Journal*, *Time* magazine, *Newsweek*, and news programs from ABC, CBS, NBC, Fox, and PBS.

---

2   http://dailycaller.com/2010/08/28/obama-democrats-got-88-percent-of-2008-contributions-by-tv-network-execs-writers-reporters/

3   http://www.businessinsider.com/proof-of-liberal-bias-in-hollywood-media-and-academia-2014-11

4   http://archive.mrc.org/books/wmd_excerpt.asp

5   http://newsroom.ucla.edu/releases/Media-Bias-Is-Real-Finds-UCLA-6664

It is no secret where Fox News lands on the political spectrum. Its ratings have topped television media not necessarily for news coverage quality (though full disclosure, if not already apparent, I appreciate it) but because it essentially has a monopoly of right-leaning broadcast within television news media. It differentiates itself from the left-leaning pack by covering the spectrum of relevant news but headlining and probing more deeply into issues newsworthy from a conservative perspective (as outlined throughout this book). As a result, it is reasonable to interpret Fox News' "fair and balanced" slogan as more appropriate in the context of its attempt to fairly balance the general cable news and mainstream media landscape. It certainly does make a solid effort, but being the only one of its kind does not balance the overall significantly left-leaning news media bias.

Beyond news sources, media bias extends into the pop-cultural worlds of entertainment on screen and in print. Celebrities, including the fanfare multiplier effect which comes with them, are cherished by liberal politicians. Liberal celebrities (redundant) offer money, faces, voices, movies, and social media presence in support of liberal politicians and causes (e.g., Lena Dunham on her *"First Time"* with President Obama, Zach Galafanakis' *Between Two Ferns* with President Obama, Kim Kardashian tweeting photos with presidential candidate Hillary Clinton). With regard to Hollywood connections, Michelle Obama sensibly told *Entertainment Tonight* during the 2012 presidential campaign, "This is going to be a close one so we are going to welcome any and everyone who wants to step up and support the progress that we've made."[6] Many Democratic fundraisers, especially those supporting Obama's campaigns,

---

6   http://www.cbspressexpress.com/cbs-television-distribution/releases/view?id=32082

are as well-attended as a glitzy Hollywood red carpet event. Celebrities such as Sarah Jessica Parker, Mariah Carey, George Clooney, and Jay-Z help contribute tens of millions of dollars[7][8] and more importantly, star-studded associations which translate to their fan bases' votes. While it is anyone's right to publicly and financially support who and how they want (apparently unless you are a wealthy conservative supporting Republicans[9]), it is problematic when a young, apolitical population views pop-culture celebrities, who are largely extraneous (PC for "naive") to the world of economic and public policy, as a primary source of political inspiration. In addition to inspiring support for liberal causes, these celebrities also inspire hostility toward conservatives through publicized distortion (e.g., Scarlett Johansson, Eva Longoria, and Kerry Washington on candidate Mitt Romney's war on women[10]) and personal dislike of those with differing opinions (e.g., Ben Affleck personifying the hypocrisy of the liberal's open mind, stating his predetermination that he would not like someone who is Republican[11]).

Celebrity support of liberal politics is widespread in print media as well. Magazine publishing continues to play a

---

[7]   https://www.washingtonpost.com/blogs/reliable-source/
       post/obamas-new-celebrity-fundraising-trick-pick-your-own-
       star/2012/06/13/gJQACs0oaV_blog.html
[8]   https://www.washingtonpost.com/politics/decision2012/jay-z-
       beyonce-raise-money-for-obama/2012/09/18/7a8e1190-01f7-11e2-
       b257-e1c2b3548a4a_story.html
[9]   http://www.usnews.com/news/the-report/articles/2015/06/26/the-
       koch-brothers-gifts-to-society
[10]   http://www.eonline.com/news/354059/scarlett-johansson-kerry-
       washington-eva-longoria-and-more-want-you-to-vote-obama
[11]   http://www.huffingtonpost.com/2013/12/09/ben-affleck-
       republicans_n_4413293.html

role in influencing popular culture and opinion. The liberal likes of Gwyneth Paltrow and Leonardo DiCaprio join the Obamas and the Clintons in gracing the covers of titles such as *Vogue*, *Glamour*, *GQ*, *Esquire*, *Rolling Stone*, *Town & Country*, and so on. Magazines have the ability to make fashion and entertainment audiences suddenly privy to *editorially-selected* political information at the flip of a page. In similar style to the rest of mainstream media, these titles offer an outlet for left-leaning undertones and overtones, at times with the editors' favorite "fabulous" liberal political faces on the cover. We are pretty confident that Anna Wintour, editor-in-chief of American *Vogue* and a *fabulously* generous supporter of the Obamas and Clintons, has no plans of giving cover-time or solid messaging opportunity to a "fabulous" conservative-minded personality (but perhaps she is of the opinion there is no such thing). However, recognition goes to *Vanity Fair* for giving the July 2015 cover to a conservative celebrity — Caitlyn Jenner.[12]

Finally, academia, a form of media within the walls of university campuses, is ripe with liberal professors and teaching assistants voicing ideological concerns and ideals to a wide student audience. This in and of itself is not necessarily the issue. Academia, just as in some other industries, typically attracts certain political persuasions for employment (e.g., conservatives to military, liberals to entertainment). However, the political-academia controversy rears its head when ideology is professed as fact to many young and impressionable minds. Any student who may be subjected to such "facts" will take one of four avenues: agree, learn to agree, superficially "agree", or dissent. Dissenting is tough, though, when a liberal professor

---

[12]   http://www.washingtonpost.com/news/the-fix/wp/2015/06/02/is-caitlyn-jenner-still-a-republican-and-is-that-even-fair-to-ask/

holds the fate of your GPA, and liberal peers influence the inclusion of your social experience. Outside the classroom experience, universities are unofficial headquarters of left-wing activist demonstrations and protests. New York University-based psychologist Jonathan Haidt, a self-described centrist, has compared the experience of being a conservative graduate student to being a closeted gay student in the 1980s.[13] Nevertheless there are many liberals who minimize claims of academia bias, seeing it as yet another right-wing myth. Rather, they believe conservatives do all the discriminating and that we are the only group who cannot be on the receiving end of discrimination — that thought in and of itself is discriminatory. Harvey Mansfield, a conservative professor of government at Harvard, argues that the anti-conservative bias is real and pronounced, saying that conservatism is "just not a respectable position to hold," where Republicans are caricatured unfavorably.[14]

In addition to academia's support of liberal ideology, the field also boldly demonstrates condemnation of anyone speaking against their "truths" protected by left-wing ideology. For example, Brandeis University's administration retracted its invitation to Ayaan Hirsi Ali for speaking out against radical facets of Islam (of which she physically endured and bravely escaped); and, Rutgers University students successfully protested a scheduled graduation speech by Condoleezza Rice, Secretary of State under the George W. Bush administration. The non-liberal messages of these significant figures overpower the fact that they are amazingly accomplished black women — a

13 http://www.washingtontimes.com/news/2012/aug/1/liberal-majority-on-campus-yes-were-biased/?page=all
14 http://www.washingtontimes.com/news/2012/aug/1/liberal-majority-on-campus-yes-were-biased/?page=all

conservative message just cannot catch a break! Juxtapose this with former Iranian President Ahmadinejad who spoke at Columbia University. He is a radical supporter of wiping Israel off the map (see Israel section) and his country, under sharia law, calls for homosexuality punishable by death.[15] The announcement of his visit was met with protesters; however, their outcries were not compelling enough to warrant an ousting as that which took place against Ali and Rice. Were these cases of selective racism or sexism, or just a case of a hypocritical liberalism displaying intolerance and closed-mindedness? The hypocrisy is blatant.

Free-ish Speech

Controversial expression is inevitable, subjective, often offensive and potentially inspirational. Given the fluid nature of controversial communication, we appreciate that our Founding Fathers addressed and protected free speech first and foremost in the U.S. Constitution. We believe in the constitutional equally protected right to free speech over what has become selective progressive-endorsed "free" speech. Sadly, we have more recently and frequently seen the First Amendment coming under attack.

It is generally assumed that the First Amendment's right to free speech has bipartisan support. Support from the Left is unmistakable, as seen and heard in various established liberal-backed demonstrations (e.g., Occupy Wall Street,

---

15   https://www.washingtonpost.com/news/worldviews/wp/2014/02/24/here-are-the-10-countries-where-homosexuality-may-be-punished-by-death/

Black Lives Matter, anti-war protests, anti-anything rallies on college campuses). However, the Left has also demonstrated an unabashed hypocrisy as it relates to free speech rights for anyone not sharing its views. In the eyes of liberalism's *selective* right to free speech, conservative speech seems automatically discounted as hate speech or "appropriation" and should be silenced. As the self-identified arbiters of political correctness and what constitutes "fair," liberals influence the free speech selection bias as they subjectively deem appropriate. To illustrate, note a recent current events sampling of the striking dichotomy between where free speech is and is not tolerated:

> In 2014 Sony Pictures launched trailers for *The Interview*, a comedy satirizing the assassination plot of the North Korean dictator Kim Jung Un. In response, the North Korean government made its disapproval of the film known by making threats against the video's release. Many Americans dismissed the threats and a liberal White House administration publicly defended the film on the grounds of freedom of speech and artistic expression. Sony Pictures' e-mail accounts and cyber-systems were subsequently hacked, and North Korea was blamed for the hacking job. The film was ultimately released with the publicized approval of President Obama.[16]

> Just two years earlier, in 2012, an Egyptian-born Coptic Christian American independently produced a 14-minute YouTube video patronizing the Islamic prophet. The same White House administration,

---

[16]   http://www.bbc.com/news/world-us-canada-30594820

which assertively stood up for a Hollywood mock assassination of a North Korean ruler on the basis of free speech, called this particular video "disgusting and reprehensible."[17] Beyond that, they blamed the video and its producer for causing the September 11, 2012, Benghazi terror attacks, in which Islamic extremists burned an American embassy and murdered four Americans. The terrorists' retaliation in the form of quadruple murder certainly makes the alleged North Korean cyber-hack retaliation a joke. Nevertheless, then-Secretary of State Hillary Clinton's "disgusting and reprehensible" comment was made in regard to the controversial *filmmaker*, not the *terrorizing murderers*. At a much later time, the White House administration revealed that the Benghazi attack was actually planned and premeditated by organized terrorists, rather than spontaneously provoked by the video. The accusation that the video was the cause of the Benghazi attacks was withdrawn,[18] albeit much less forcefully than it was alleged.

In 2011 producers of *South Park* produced a Broadway musical entitled *The Book of Mormon*. The musical, not unlike its popular sister production, serves as a comedic mockery of religion. While many could rightfully claim that *South Park* is, for better or worse (I'd support for the better), an equal opportunity satirical offender, the same cannot be said about *The Book of*

---

[17]   http://www.americanthinker.com/articles/2012/09/hillary_cheered_broadways_book_of_mormon_condemns_innocence_of_muslims.html

[18]   http://www.factcheck.org/2012/10/benghazi-timeline/

Mormon. In addition to serving as the musical's feature headline title, Mormons and Mormon traditions are clearly singled-out, mocked, and disparaged in ways ranging from "playful" to explicitly crass. The producers and fans of the musical defend accusations of religious bigotry by claiming that *The Book of Mormon* purely serves as a model of the ridiculousness behind *all* formalized religions.[19] Based on the producers' track record of equal opportunity discrimination, this might well be their truth. However, what would the industry and public response be if this *same* Broadway musical, allegedly representing all religions, was instead titled *The Book of Koran*? Would the same show still receive the same sold-out fanfare, Tony Awards, and praise, including applause from Hillary Clinton?[20] How would a liberal White House administration react? "Artistic expression" or "reprehensible"? The blatant hypocrisies in today's pop-political culture have come to outweigh the issue of controversial content.

Controversy surrounding speech, writing, and art has always been an intensely debated matter. Controversial expression has been an issue for as long as expression has been free to exercise, and the subjects of such expressions have long been equally targeted. Many of these expressions can be absolutely appalling, with passionate protests and heated reactions being reasonable as well as expected.

---

19   http://www.deseretnews.com/article/865633823/Why-The-Book-of-Mormon-musical-is-not-just-offensive-2-its-shallow.html?pg=all

20   http://www.americanthinker.com/articles/2012/09/hillary_cheered_broadways_book_of_mormon_condemns_innocence_of_muslims.html

In 1977 the neo-Nazi Ku Klux Klan announced its plan to march with the swastika in the predominantly Jewish town of Skokie, Illinois (home to many Holocaust survivors). The Supreme Court ruled against the town's protest and in favor of the KKK on the grounds of free speech.[21] Ultimately, the march took place in Chicago rather than Skokie.

In 1987 an artist's photograph of a crucified Jesus in a jar of his urine, titled "Piss Christ," was awarded government grants (though awards were later retracted on the grounds of constitutional separation of church and state[22]); then in 2012 the artwork was prominently re-featured in a New York City museum (not without protests, of course).[23]

In 2015 the Jihad Watch hosted a "Muhammad Art Exhibit and Cartoon Contest," with a $10,000 prize going to the winning cartoon depicting the prophet Muhammed. An admittedly provocative response to then-recent Charlie Hebdo massacres, the event in Garland, Texas, carried on despite town objections over blasphemy and safety concerns.[24]

Examples of blatantly incendiary free speech demonstrate that exercising the right to it is not always civil or sensible, but it is

---

[21] http://caselaw.findlaw.com/us-supreme-court/432/43.html

[22] http://www.firstamendmentcenter.org/public-funding-of-controversial-art

[23] http://www.theguardian.com/artanddesign/2012/sep/28/andres-serrano-piss-christ-new-york

[24] https://www.washingtonpost.com/news/morning-mix/wp/2015/05/04/why-a-woman-named-pamela-geller-organized-a-prophet-muhammad-cartoon-contest/

a necessary subjective frustration if we are to constitutionally uphold it. However, hypocritical discrimination around free speech has become a relatively new and extremely unreasonable epidemic: from college campuses ousting professors and administrators for "culturally appropriating" students' "safe space,"[25] to attempted murders in response to the aforementioned "Muhammad Art Exhibit and Cartoon Contest." It is evident to us that the right to free speech is selectively respected depending on who you are or whom you are offending. In other words, the right to freely express controversial content is becoming selectively applied in today's pop-politicized PC culture. Even though the right to free speech legally remains, it is increasingly becoming an uncomfortable basic right to exercise.

Applicable Extremism

Extremists exist in just about every group. An extremist embodies the most concentrated version, typically in the negative sense, of a given demographic. An extremist is also among the most expressive via words or actions given his or her "extreme" passion for a cause. In light of recent religiously- and racially-charged events, liberals have insistently espoused the message that it is wrong to make blanket generalizations based on extremists' actions: from Islamic terrorists who do not represent the true religion of Islam, to violent rioters who infiltrate but do not represent Black Lives Matter demonstrations. We agree with these sentiments:

---

[25] http://www.usnews.com/news/the-report/articles/2015/11/25/from-megaphones-to-muzzles-free-speech-safe-spaces-and-college-campuses

generalizations should not be made based on the behavior of extremists. However, we are personally aware of the hypocrisies which lie under a veil of nondiscrimination espoused by some liberals. If only they would apply this line of reason to politics, then liberal pop-political culture would not be so scathingly judgmental of conservatives — and perhaps would be open to hearing opposing rationales.

When conservatives are characterized by extremist caricatures or attacked with vulgar extremist references, where are the liberals condemning the injustice? Ironically, many liberals are the ones throwing it our way. A cultural trend (i.e., pop-political culture) has manifested whereby it is *not* discriminatory, (rather, it's humorous and generates "Likes") to denigrate conservatives with name-calling and accusations ranging from extreme generalizations to flagrantly false statements. This is certainly not to say that conservatives are free from blame in the dirty game of political mudslinging. But fortunately for liberals and unfortunately for conservatives, liberalism has the backing of Hollywood heavy hitters, pop-culture celebrities, as well as others within mainstream and social media to perpetuate a narrative — in this case, that we are the extremist caricature. Inherent to their professional skills, these powerful vocal supporters are able to create a brand image of liberalism as the party of openness (except to conservatives) and selfless generosity (often in the form of generously tweeted selfies). This is surely anyone's right to identify with a political belief and espouse it as seen fit. In the spirit of conservatism, good for anyone who utilizes their abilities to achieve a goal — in this case, to influence support of liberalism. However, doing this by propagating that extremism comprehensively applies to conservatism in a way unlike other demographics is dishonest and hypocritical.

So while the liberal fantasy is that conservatism *is* extremism, the conservative reality is liberals (e.g., media, celebrities, colleges) influence pop-political culture. We have come to know this to be quite annoying. But the other part of our reality is that their influence is only as effective as we allow it to be. As intimidating as it may be, by personally utilizing our conservative belief in the individual we can collectively counter their influence. Conservatives do not have the star-studded support as those backing liberals, so the charge is on us to become more confident in representing our mainstream bleeding heart conservatism.

THE OBJECTIVE

Among the field of 2016 GOP primary candidates at the time of this writing, we have seen that key conservative initiatives are shared by the field: strengthening our national security, invigorating the economy, championing the individual, safeguarding equal opportunity, etc. These positions resonate with a considerable portion of the American people as evidenced by a Republican-controlled House and Senate. So why does it still feel like we are the underdogs for this upcoming presidential election?

Moody's Analytics, which boasts a perfect record in predicting every presidential race since Reagan's first term, announced that 2016 will once again favor the Democrats.[1] One crucial determinant of this outcome is voter turnout, which is consistently and significantly lower for midterm elections versus presidential elections.[2] I facetiously attribute the higher turnout largely to celebrities who decide every four years that they are now politically inclined. Unfortunately for Republican candidates, endorsements from the famous and beautiful skew Left. Kate McKinnon, portraying Ann Romney during a *Saturday Night Live* sketch, put it best by saying, "If you're a Democrat,

---

[1]   https://www.economy.com/dismal/analysis/commentary/255843/A-NailBiter-in-2016/

[2]   http://www.pewresearch.org/fact-tank/2014/07/24/voter-turnout-always-drops-off-for-midterm-elections-but-why/

you get to eat with the cool people like George Clooney. If you're a Republican, you get to shake Jon Voight's cold lizard hands." Thankfully, our Founding Fathers had the foresight to ensure that my vote and yours count every bit as much as Kim Kardashian's and Kanye West's. However, you and I alone probably can't reach the same size audience as "Kimye."

You may not have agreed with every position presented in this book, and I can respect that. But if you agree with many of these views and have come to these conclusions through a rational, fair-minded thought process, I would call you a fellow Bleeding Heart Conservative. And it is on us, as responsible citizens with a sense of civic duty, to initiate a rebranding of the Republican Party. Alas, this turnaround of the public's perception will not come simply by way of a Katy Perry endorsement. The support has to come from ourselves and each other — a kind of grassroots stance against distorted and outright false attacks coming from the Left (see Appendix).

I firmly believe that Republicans face a branding issue and *not* a principles issue. We know that at its core, our party remains on the right track to reverse the fiscal, social, and foreign policy failures we have witnessed over the past several years. Our political philosophy is based on core fundamentals involving freedom, independence, equality, and opportunity in the interest of empowering the individual. Bleeding heart conservatives, in particular, have the voice to contribute to rebranding, through representing and articulating the conservative reality for what it is — good! As evidenced in this book, our politics and policy beliefs hold no malice or bigotry. After outlining the variety of core issues in current-day politics and presenting BHC positions, I hope that I have conveyed the way compassion manifests itself in conservative philosophy. Anyone who is open to accepting the truth about honest conservatism, regardless of personal political opinion, will understand that political diversity does not have to lead to political divisiveness.

If we want non-conservatives to be open to at least listening before judging — the policy *and* the person — we need to garner the confidence and willingness to voice our right-leaning ideas when relevant conversation calls for it (for example, with left-leaning family members, friends, colleagues, and neighbors). After all, a core tenet of liberalism is having an open mind towards others' opinions and beliefs — let's be a driving influence to remind liberals that it's okay to include conservatives in their tolerance. When this occurs, once taboo discussions can become less confrontational and more enlightening, with less emotion and more ideas. Through openly identifying our political thought, we humanize the party. From here we may elaborate on why we lean right and how we believe conservative principles are the best vehicle for solutions to improve our communities, society, and the world. By defeating liberal intimidation, real conservatism will remain relevant and be able to expand its positive influence to benefit *everyone*.

With the support of the BHC voice and presence, conservative values can move into the White House via a Republican president who understands that the office must champion the individual primarily through keeping government overreach in check and American security protected. I am optimistic that this will propel the conservative brand into a new chapter in the eyes of American culture. Fittingly for a conservative movement, this responsibility falls on the individual. I hope you, too, will participate.

APPENDIX

Popular Slander-Turned-Popular "Truth"

"The Conservatives' war on women" — *False*
- ° Conservatives absolutely support equality and empowerment of women — educationally, professionally, financially, politically, maternally, and socially; that said, we support empowerment for people of all genders, races, religions, ethnicities, and otherwise
- ° Conservatives support equal pay for equal work; in fact, it was Republican Congresswoman Winifred Stanley who first introduced equal pay legislation in 1944; though not until 20 years later was it finally passed with bipartisan support
- ° With regard to the abortion debate, it is key to understand that from a conservative's perspective, while specific exceptions exist, the pro-life policy focus is on the baby in utero and defending his or her unalienable and constitutional right to life

"Conservatives are anti-gay rights" — *False*
- ° Conservatives believe in equal rights for everyone regardless of sexual orientation

° With regard to marriage, many conservatives are in favor of marriage equality for same-sex couples and accept the 2015 Supreme Court decision on the matter

- Debate however, remains around the Supreme Court taking *constitutional* jurisdiction over the issue, implying marriage is a constitutional right; rather, the counterview sees the matter as constitutionally falling under congressional or state jurisdiction (the dissenting opinion shared by four of the nine Supreme Court judges hearing this landmark case)

° A religious subset of conservatives upholds the traditional definition of marriage which is of religious origin — that is, marriage is between a man and woman; many conservatives believe there is a place for traditional religious marriages and an equal place for civil/secular/same-sex religious marriages; our secular government recognizes both

"Conservatives are anti-immigration" — *False*

° Conservatives wholeheartedly support legal, documented immigrants, especially those who aspire to achieve the American dream

° Conservatives oppose illegal undocumented immigration, just as we oppose any illegal action or practice

° Conservatives want to reform the immigration system so that well-intentioned and earnest foreigners can be documented (just as we all are) so they may equitably and safely live and work in the U.S.; at the same time, such reforms will make

dishonest and dangerous foreigners unable or reluctant to illegally enter
- Conservatives believe thorough border control is especially necessary at the present time given the extreme terror threats our country faces

"Conservatives oppose voting rights" — False
° Conservatives support and encourage every American citizen to register to vote and legally exercise the right to vote
° Conservatives are against fraudulent votes, including voting under another registered citizen's identification — for this reason we support proof of photo ID at the voting booth
° Similar to a moderate liberal's view on gun rights, conservatives believe that exercising the constitutional right to vote should be qualified by adequate background checks to preserve greater lawfulness

"Conservatives oppose increases for minimum wage workers" — False
° Conservatives support providing minimum wage workers with opportunities (e.g., better quality jobs, job training, promotions) to lift themselves to increased salaries
° Conservatives support incentivizing employers to recognize valued employees with raises and promotions
° Conservatives support keeping a minimum wage level appropriate for young, new, unskilled workers

- ° Conservatives oppose the unintended consequences of federally mandated wage increases which negatively impact workers, employers, and the overall economy
  - Elicits an unfavorable economic cycle returning low-income workers back to unfavorable circumstances
    - Mandated uneconomical wage hikes → consumer price increases → unhealthy inflation → reduced consumption → business stagnation → job cuts → reduced consumption → business stagnation à more job cuts...

"Conservatives oppose paying their fair share" — False
- ° Conservatives support paying a fair share in taxes to contribute to funding essential public programs and initiatives
- ° Conservatives support all citizens keeping their fair share of their earned income to utilize as they see appropriate: spend, invest, save, donate (all economically-productive activities)
- ° Conservatives oppose big government divisively defining the concept of "fair," pitting lower-income workers against higher-income workers with nothing productive to show for it (unless Occupy Wall Streeters were considered productive)
  - Elicits a vicious cycle of tax increases with insufficient or unsustainable societal benefit (rather, societal damage, including resentment among income classes)
    - Societal problems exist → big government requires taxpayer money

to fund programs to fix problems → if societal problems not resolved or worsen then → big government taxes higher earners to pay more to fund programs to fix problems → if societal problems not resolved or worsen then → big government blames higher earners for not paying their fair share to fix problems...

- Note Albert Einstein's definition of insanity: doing the same thing over and over again and expecting different results;[1] conservatives would like the government to recognize that more money does not necessarily fix a problem — this may feel good but does not always do good

° Many conservatives believe a flat tax rate, where everyone pays the same percentage of his or her income, is the purest form of "fair"; under this plan higher earners would always pay much more in taxes than lower earners

---

[1] http://www.brainyquote.com/quotes/quotes/a/alberteins133991.html

ABOUT THE AUTHOR

Allison Lee Pillinger Choi was born and raised in South Florida where she was taught the principles of hard work, patience, respect, and accountability—the same qualities she sees as the fundamentals of conservatism. She witnessed first-hand what such principles can realize as her parents progressed from working class to middle class and eventually to upper middle class. Her mother, a Korean-born American immigrant, moved to the U.S. to live and work in a meritocratic society where women and men are viewed as equals. Her father, a Brooklyn-born third generation Jewish American immigrant, served as a U.S. Navy pilot, later becoming a Delta Airlines Captain and finally a charter school teacher upon retirement from aviation. Alli went on to Harvard where she concentrated in Economics, competed on the NCAA Division I Varsity tennis team, and worked at *The Harvard Crimson*. At Harvard she was surprised by both bias in favor of liberalism and bias against conservatism, especially coming from the swing state of Florida where diverse opinion is more pervasive. After graduating she moved to New York City, still another bastion of liberalism, where she worked as an analyst at Goldman Sachs and then Equinox. She has also contributed her time to the non-profit organization New York Cares, the New York Hospital Weill Cornell Council, the Women's National Republican Club, and the Manhattan Institute Young Leaders Circle. Now a full-time mom, Alli lives with her husband, toddler, and infant in New York City.